MR A'S AMAZING
MAZE PLAYS

ALAN AYCKBOURN

faber and faber

LONDON · BOSTON

First published in 1989
by Faber and Faber Limited
3 Queen Square London WC1N 3AU

Printed in Great Britain by
Richard Clay Ltd, Bungay, Suffolk

© Haydonning Ltd, 1989

All rights whatsoever in this play are strictly
reserved and applications for permission to
perform it, etc. must be made in advance, before
rehearsals begin, to Margaret Ramsay Ltd,
14a Goodwins Court, St Martin's Lane,
London WC2N 4LL

A CIP record for this book is available
from the British Library.

ISBN 0-571-14160-9

Mr A's Amazing Maze Plays was first performed at the Stephen Joseph Theatre in the Round, Scarborough, on 30 November 1988.

The cast was as follows:

SUZY	Kerry Peers
NEVILLE, her dog	Adam Godley
MOTHER	Victoria Carling
FATHER	Richard Brain
MR ACCOUSTICUS	Roger Forbes
MR PASSERBY	John Branwell
1st NARRATOR	Graeme Eton
2nd NARRATOR	Philip Fox

Director	Alan Ayckbourn
Assistant Director	Stephen Mallatratt
Designer	Michael Holt
Costumes	Laura McLaughlin
Lighting	Mick Thomas

Scene: In and around Suzy's cottage. Mr Accousticus's house.

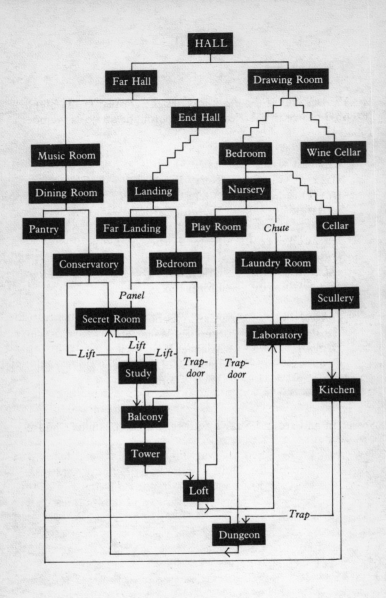

PART I

Scene: a set that can be used for a lot of different places: levels and steps. The two NARRATORS *enter. They greet the audience.*

1ST NARRATOR: This is the story of a girl called Suzy . . .
(*Light up on* SUZY.)

2ND NARRATOR: Suzy didn't think of herself as very brave but in this story she turns out to be very brave indeed.

1ST NARRATOR: Suzy didn't think of herself as very special either, but in this story she turns out to be very special indeed.

2ND NARRATOR: And that's the story we're going to tell you today.

1ST NARRATOR: Suzy lived with her mother in a small village somewhere quite near here.
(*Light up on* MOTHER.)

2ND NARRATOR: Suzy's mother was very kind. But because she had to go out to work in a biscuit shop every day to earn the money to feed them both and because she had to spend the rest of the time cooking and washing and looking after Suzy – she was often very tired . . .

1ST NARRATOR: Although Suzy would help her mother whenever she could. Well, when she remembered to . . .

2ND NARRATOR: You see, Suzy used to have a father but not any more.

1ST NARRATOR: When she was still very young he'd taken part in a balloon race. Only something had gone wrong with his balloon and instead of coming down at the end of the race, he'd gone up and up and up and up and nobody's ever seen him again.

2ND NARRATOR: Suzy often thought about her father and felt very sad. But because she'd been so young when he'd gone, she could hardly remember him any more.

1ST NARRATOR: Suzy's mother missed him, though. Sometimes, when she was in bed, Suzy could hear her crying. And that made Suzy sad, all over again.

2ND NARRATOR: Suzy had no brothers and sisters . . .

1ST NARRATOR: And although she went to school, she didn't have any really special friends.

2ND NARRATOR: Because although her mother worked very hard all day, they still didn't have very much money. And most of the other children at her school were rather rich and their parents didn't like them to play with children as poor as Suzy.

1ST NARRATOR: So for a long time she was very lonely. Which worried Suzy's mother because she was, as we've said, very kind . . .

2ND NARRATOR: So her mother saved up some money, secretly, and one day, when it was Suzy's birthday, she brought her a very special present.

(MOTHER *enters with a small shoe box with holes punched in the lid. She gives it to* SUZY.)

1ST NARRATOR: Suzy couldn't think what it could be.

(SUZY *opens the box. A small puppy (glove puppet) sticks its head out of the box.*)

SUZY: (*Delighted*) It's a puppy!

2ND NARRATOR: Suzy was overjoyed.

MOTHER: Now look after him, Suzy. He's your very own puppy and you must take extra special care of him because he's very small.

SUZY: I'll take care of him for ever and ever –

1ST NARRATOR: Said Suzy.

2ND NARRATOR: Because, truthfully, he was a very, very small puppy indeed.

MOTHER: What are you going to call him?

1ST NARRATOR: Asked her mother.

2ND NARRATOR: And Suzy thought and thought and thought. She thought of Fido . . .

SUZY: No . . .

1ST NARRATOR: And she thought of Fred . . .

SUZY: No . . .

2ND NARRATOR: And she thought of Rags . . .

1ST NARRATOR: And Rastus . . .

2ND NARRATOR: And Rover . . .

1ST NARRATOR: And Spot . . .

2ND NARRATOR: And Smudge . . .

1ST NARRATOR: And Prince . . .

2ND NARRATOR: And Patch . . .

1ST NARRATOR: And Dylan . . .

2ND NARRATOR: And Digby . . .

1ST NARRATOR: And Lucky . . .

2ND NARRATOR: And Lupus . . .

1ST NARRATOR: And Bonzo . . .

2ND NARRATOR: And Bones . . .

(SUZY *shakes her head at all these suggestions.*)

1ST NARRATOR: And nothing seemed to fit.

MOTHER: Well, he has to have a name . . .

2ND NARRATOR: Said her mother . . .

1ST NARRATOR: And Suzy said –

SUZY: *I* know . . .

1ST NARRATOR: ⎫
2ND NARRATOR: ⎬ (*Together*) What?
MOTHER: ⎭

SUZY: I'll call him Neville.

1ST NARRATOR: ⎫
2ND NARRATOR: ⎬ (*Together*) Neville!
MOTHER: ⎭

SUZY: Neville.

MOTHER: I don't think that's a very good name for a puppy, dear.

SUZY: He's my puppy, you told me he was, and that's what I want to call him.

1ST NARRATOR: And so Neville he was called.

2ND NARRATOR: It was certainly a very strange name for a very small dog.

1ST NARRATOR: From that day on, everywhere that Suzy went, Neville went. He was so small she could even take him to school with her in the box and hide him in her desk.

2ND NARRATOR: Until, that is, he started eating her pencils and her school books and then they were both sent home.

1ST NARRATOR: Neville liked eating.

2ND NARRATOR: He liked sleeping, too . . .

1ST NARRATOR: But best of all, he liked eating. He ate everything. Shoes and chairs and curtains and cushions.

2ND NARRATOR: But he never tried to eat Suzy . . .

3

1ST NARRATOR: . . . because she was very gentle with him. When Suzy was at home, Neville would sit in her pocket all day, just happy to be with her.

2ND NARRATOR: And at night he would sleep in his box at the foot of her bed.

1ST NARRATOR: As the months went by, Neville kept eating and eating and growing and growing.

2ND NARRATOR: So that very soon he had stopped being a puppy and become a small dog.
(MOTHER *crosses with a bigger cardboard box.*)

1ST NARRATOR: And Suzy's mother brought her home a bigger box for Neville to sleep in . . .

SUZY: (*As she goes off*) Here we are, Neville . . . Here's a lovely new box for you . . .

2ND NARRATOR: Very soon after that, Neville stopped being a small dog . . .

1ST NARRATOR: . . . and grew into a very big dog indeed . . .
(SUZY *staggers back across with a huge box.*)

SUZY: (*As she goes off*) Here you are, Neville . . . Here's a lovely new box for you . . .

2ND NARRATOR: Until finally there was no room in their tiny cottage for Suzy and her mother and Neville all to sleep there.

1ST NARRATOR: And Suzy's mother said:

MOTHER: Suzy, Neville is going to have to sleep in the yard from now on . . .

SUZY: Oh . . .

MOTHER: I'm sorry, I'm not having that dog in the house at night. He's far too BIG.

SUZY: But, Mum, what if it rains?

MOTHER: If it rains he can sleep on the porch.

SUZY: But, Mum, what if it's cold?

MOTHER: Then we'll find him something warm to sleep on. I know. He can have that old cellulellular blanket.
(MOTHER *goes inside the house.*)

2ND NARRATOR: Actually, what Suzy's mother meant to say was cellular blanket. She was quite clever really, but for some reason she often got words wrong.

SUZY: (*Calling*) Neville, come on, boy. Out here then, Neville, come on.
 (NEVILLE *comes out. He is a very big dog indeed.*)
1ST NARRATOR: He was a sort of Old English Wolf Boxer.
NEVILLE: Woof!
SUZY: Come on, Neville.
NEVILLE: Woof!
SUZY: Shhh! That's enough.
 (NEVILLE *jumps up and puts his paws on Suzy's shoulders and licks her face. She is knocked over by the sheer weight of him.*)
 Neville! Don't do that!
2ND NARRATOR: And he did have a magnificent bark!
NEVILLE: (*Loudly*) WOOF!
SUZY: SSSHHH!
1ST NARRATOR: Though it was sometimes rather loud.
NEVILLE: (*Quieter*) WOOF!
SUZY: Sssh!
NEVILLE: (*Very quietly*) Woof!
SUZY: Now, Neville, you're going to have to sleep out here tonight.
 (NEVILLE *whimpers.*)
 Yes, well, I'm sorry. That's the way it has to be.
 (NEVILLE *whimpers again.*)
 Now, don't be silly. I'll come and sit out here with you until you're asleep.
 (*Another moan from* NEVILLE.)
 A big dog like you can't be frightened of the dark. And you're just under my window so I won't be far away.
 (*Resigned noise from* NEVILLE. MOTHER *comes out of the house with a blanket.*)
MOTHER: Here you are, Neville. Here's a nice warm cellulellular blanket for you.
SUZY: Can he have a hot-water bottle?
MOTHER: No, of course he can't. Whatever next? Whoever heard of a dog sleeping with a hot-water bottle? Don't be so silly, Suzy.
 (MOTHER *goes inside.*)
SUZY: (*Softly, to* NEVILLE) If it gets cold in the night, I'll bring you a hot-water bottle, Neville.

(NEVILLE *licks her.*)

Now settle down, Neville.

(SUZY *spreads out the blanket for* NEVILLE *to lie on.* NEVILLE *crawls underneath it and appears the other side. He lies with just his nose sticking out.* SUZY *sits by him. The lights change under the next.*)

1ST NARRATOR: As they sat together in the back yard and watched the sun set, they saw the moon rise and all the stars come out.

2ND NARRATOR: And they did what they often did. They both stared up into the night sky to see if there was any sign, any sign at all of Suzy's father, who was probably still up there in his balloon.

1ST NARRATOR: But there was nobody in sight.

SUZY: (*Sadly*) Nobody.

(NEVILLE *howls softly.*)

2ND NARRATOR: And Suzy started remembering the last time she had seen her father. It was the day he'd set out to take part in The Great International Balloon Race.

(*Sunlight.*)

1ST NARRATOR: It had been a lovely day. The sun had been shining. The band was playing.

(*Band music.*)

2ND NARRATOR: The crowds were cheering.

(*Crowds cheering.*)

1ST NARRATOR: A perfect day for The Great International Balloon Race.

(MOTHER *has joined* SUZY *as part of the crowd.* MOTHER *gives* SUZY *one of two small Union Jacks. Both wave their flags and cheer.*)

2ND NARRATOR: And here comes Suzy's father now.

(FATHER *appears. He is dressed in a flying coat, leather helmet and goggles. He looks a real hero. The crowd go wild. He waves to them, cheerfully.*)

1ST NARRATOR: He was very, very popular with the crowd.

2ND NARRATOR: They loved him.

1ST NARRATOR: But nobody loved him more than Suzy and her mother did.

(FATHER *embraces first* MOTHER *and then* SUZY.)

6

FATHER: (*As he does so, to* MOTHER) Goodbye, old love. See you soon.

MOTHER: (*Tearfully*) Be careful, Jack, be careful.

FATHER: Don't you worry about me. I'll be home by tea-time.

SUZY: Goodbye, Dad . . .

FATHER: Goodbye, Suzy. You look after your mother, now. Tell her to stop worrying.

SUZY: Dad, I . . .

(*A cannon sounds.*)

FATHER: Right, here we go. Goodbye, then.

(*The crowd roar.* FATHER *climbs aboard his balloon.* SUZY *calls to him but her voice is barely heard above the crowd.*)

SUZY: (*Calling*) Dad . . . Dad . . .

FATHER: Bye . . .

MOTHER: Goodbye, Jack. Goodbye . . .

SUZY: Dad . . . Dad . . .

(FATHER *goes.* MOTHER *and* SUZY *keep waving and calling till he's out of sight. When he's gone they both walk away. The crowd sounds fade and the lights change back to evening.* MOTHER *goes off.* SUZY *resumes her seat on the porch with* NEVILLE.)

2ND NARRATOR: And Suzy, although she shouted as loud as she could, never got the chance to tell her father how much she loved him.

SUZY: Dad . . .

1ST NARRATOR: And now he was up there somewhere in his balloon and maybe she'd never see him again to tell him. She sat there on the porch remembering all this and suddenly felt very sad.

2ND NARRATOR: And as it grew really dark, Neville fell asleep and Suzy very gently covered him up and tiptoed back into the house, so as not to wake him.

(SUZY *goes into the house.*)

1ST NARRATOR: But as soon as she'd gone, Neville was awake and alert.

(NEVILLE *sits up sharply.*)

2ND NARRATOR: Now that he was outside all night, Neville decided to become a first-class watch-dog. He watched everything very, very carefully, all night.

1ST NARRATOR: And if he saw or heard anything the least bit suspicious, he barked at it. He barked at moths . . .

NEVILLE: (*Seeing a moth*) Woof!

2ND NARRATOR: He barked at bats . . .

NEVILLE: (*Seeing a bat*) Woof!

1ST NARRATOR: He barked at owls . . .

(*Owl hoots.*)

NEVILLE: Woof!

2ND NARRATOR: He barked at cats . . .

(*Cat yowls.*)

NEVILLE: Woof! Woof!

1ST NARRATOR: And if anyone happened to pass by the house on their way home late at night from the pub . . .

(MR PASSERBY *enters, rather drunk, singing loudly.*)

MR PASSERBY: (*Singing croakily*) Early one morning,

Just as the sun was rising . . .

1ST NARRATOR: Then Neville really barked.

NEVILLE: (*Furiously*) Woof! Woof! Woof! Woof! Woof!

(MR PASSERBY *runs off, alarmed.*)

(*Pleased*) Woof!

2ND NARRATOR: And Neville settled back, pleased to think that, thanks to him, the house was perfectly safe and that Suzy and her mother could both sleep securely in their beds.

1ST NARRATOR: Although, unfortunately, because Neville made so much noise, they didn't get much sleep anyway.

SUZY: (*Calling*) Neville, shut up out there!

NEVILLE: (*Hurt*) Woof!

2ND NARRATOR: And in the mornings when Suzy had to go to school, Neville would walk all the way with her . . .

1ST NARRATOR: Though he didn't go inside with her any more. He was far too big to hide in a desk . . .

2ND NARRATOR: But in the afternoon he would come and meet her and they would walk home together.

1ST NARRATOR: In the evenings, sometimes, if it was nice weather, they'd go for walks together – or they'd play chases or hide and seek . . . Only Suzy could never hide from Neville for long . . .

(NEVILLE *covers his eyes.* SUZY *hides.*)

SUZY: (*Calling*) Ready!
(NEVILLE *snuffles about, follows her trail and quickly finds her.*)
NEVILLE: (*Pleased*) Woof!
SUZY: Oh, Neville. Your turn, then . . .
(*She covers her eyes and* NEVILLE *hides his head but not the rest of himself.*)
2ND NARRATOR: Actually, Neville wasn't very good at hiding, either.
NEVILLE: Woof!
SUZY: (*Uncovering her eyes and seeing him immediately*) Oh, Neville!
(NEVILLE *looks up surprised.*)
1ST NARRATOR: Just opposite Suzy's little cottage, there stood a great big house. It was very old and the windows were shuttered and the doors were nailed up because nobody lived there any more.
2ND NARRATOR: In fact nobody had lived there since Suzy could remember.
1ST NARRATOR: It was a very sinister house. Suzy used to imagine it was haunted. She would never go near it after dark.
2ND NARRATOR: She could see it from her bedroom window at night and sometimes she'd look out and imagine she could see people moving about in there.
1ST NARRATOR: But then she told herself it was only her imagination because the old house was, after all, perfectly empty.
(*Birdsong under the next.*)
2ND NARRATOR: But it did have a lovely big overgrown garden and when it was daylight, Neville and Suzy played in this a lot. It was very wild and like a jungle.
1ST NARRATOR: Neville liked it especially because he could imagine he was a tiger. He could hide and jump out at Suzy and pretend to attack her.
NEVILLE: (*Jumping out, loudly*) Woof!
SUZY: (*Startled*) Wah!
2ND NARRATOR: But then sometimes Suzy would do the same to Neville.

9

SUZY: Boo!

NEVILLE: (*Startled*) Woof!

1ST NARRATOR: They loved that garden. But they never went near the old house . . . and they never, never lingered after dusk.

(*Birdsong fades.* MOTHER *comes out.*)

MOTHER: Come on, you two. Time for supper. Hot buttered toast and delicious asparararararagus soup.

SUZY: (*To* NEVILLE) I think she means asparagus.

2ND NARRATOR: And sometimes, after supper and before they all went to bed, if she wasn't too tired from working in the biscuit shop, Mother would tell them stories that she'd made up herself . . .

MOTHER: Once upon a time there was a young shepherderpherd boy who fell in love with a beautiful mermermermer-maid . . .

1ST NARRATOR: The stories were sometimes a bit hard to follow . . .

2ND NARRATOR: But none the less Suzy and Neville would listen wide-eyed and if the story got particularly exciting . . .

MOTHER: And the wild wind whistled round the house and down the chimneyimney pots . . .

1ST NARRATOR: Neville would get rather carried away . . . (NEVILLE *howls.*)

SUZY: Quiet, Neville . . .

2ND NARRATOR: But the stories, like all good stories, always had a happy ending.

MOTHER: . . . and they all lived happily ever after. That's it now. Bed-time.

SUZY: Oh, no. Just one more . . .

MOTHER: Come along. That's it . . .

NEVILLE: Woof!

MOTHER: Neville! I said that's it.

SUZY: Not even a tiny, short story . . .

MOTHER: Suzy, I'm very tired. I have to get up early to go to work and you have to go to school . . . Now come along.

SUZY: I wish you didn't have to go to work . . .

MOTHER: Well, I do. Otherwise we wouldn't eat. Now don't

argue, please. You take Neville out into the yard and I'll
go and turn down your eiderdeiderdown . . .

SUZY: (*To* NEVILLE) I think she means eiderdown.

(SUZY *and* NEVILLE *move into the yard.* MOTHER *goes off.*)
I wish Mum didn't have to work so hard.

NEVILLE: (*In agreement*) Woof!

SUZY: I wish we had lots of money, then Mum wouldn't need
to . . .

NEVILLE: (*In agreement*) Woof!

SUZY: Most of all, I wish Dad was here . . .

NEVILLE: (*In agreement*) Woof!

1ST NARRATOR: And, as they always did before they went to
sleep, Suzy and Neville looked up into the night sky to
see if they could see her father.

2ND NARRATOR: But there was no sign of either him or his
balloon.

SUZY: Oh, Dad. One day, come back to us. Please come back.

(NEVILLE *howls softly. A moment. The lights brighten.*)

1ST NARRATOR: Sometimes, especially at weekends, Suzy and
Neville would go visiting. The person they liked visiting
most was their nearby neighbour, Mr Passserby.

(MR PASSERBY *enters.*)

2ND NARRATOR: Mr Passerby used to be a very famous opera
singer.

1ST NARRATOR: Or so he said . . .

2ND NARRATOR: He was known as The Great Pacerbi and he
sang in all the opera houses of the world.

1ST NARRATOR: He used to tell Suzy and Neville of his
travels . . .

MR PASSERBY: I sang in Rome, that's in Italy. I sang in Sydney.
That's in Australia. I sang in New York. That's in New
York. And I sang in Milan. That's in Greece.

SUZY: I thought Milan was in Italy.

2ND NARRATOR: Suzy was particularly good at geography.

MR PASSERBY: Yes, there's one there as well. Now, here I am
working for the council. One day they're cheering me,
throwing flowers, crowding around me for my autograph.
Now where am I? Painting white lines down the middle

of the road. Nobody wants to know me. Everyone tries to run me over. How are the mightly fallen, eh?

SUZY: Why did you stop singing, Mr Passerby?

MR PASSERBY: I lost my voice, didn't I?

SUZY: You mean you had a sore throat?

MR PASSERBY: (*Laughing bitterly*) A sore throat! You think I'd have stopped singing just because of a sore throat? No, I meant what I said. I lost my voice. My voice went, didn't it?

SUZY: Went where?

MR PASSERBY: It was stolen during the night.

SUZY: Stolen?

MR PASSERBY: While I was sleeping in Paris. Or perhaps it was Portugal. Peru, perhaps. Someone broke into my room while I was peacefully sleeping and stole my voice.

SUZY: How? How do you steal a voice?

MR PASSERBY: Same as you steal anything. They crept in and they reached down my throat and very, very carefully took out my voice without even waking me up. Extremely skilful. Let that be a warning to you, Suzy. And you, Neville. Never sleep with your mouth open. Do you sleep with your mouth open?

SUZY: I don't know. I'm asleep.

MR PASSERBY: You want to do what I do, these days. When I go to bed now, I always sleep with an orange under my chin. Like that, you see. Helps to keep my mouth shut. In case he tries again.

SUZY: Who?

MR PASSERBY: The voice stealer.

SUZY: But if someone stole your voice, how can you still talk?

MR PASSERBY: Because he was clever, wasn't he? He not only stole my real voice. He left me this voice instead. But this isn't my real voice.

SUZY: It isn't?

1ST NARRATOR: Suzy was finding this particular story of Mr Passerby's rather hard to believe.

NEVILLE: Woof!

2ND NARRATOR: So was Neville.

MR PASSERBY: No. This is an old, second-hand voice. I could

12

never have sung with this voice. I could never have filled an opera house with a voice like this . . . (*Demonstrating croakily*) Do . . . ray . . . me . . . fa . . . so . . . la . . . te . . . do . . .

(NEVILLE *joins in, howling*.)

Listen to that. I ask you. Even the dog hates it.

1ST NARRATOR: Suzy was very kind-hearted, though.

SUZY: It's quite a nice voice, Mr Passerby.

MR PASSERBY: It's terrible. I hate it.

SUZY: Where do you think your real voice is?

MR PASSERBY: I don't know. Somebody's got it. Somewhere. Whenever there's an opera on the radio or the TV, I always listen. Hoping I might recognize it. But it's impossible. I think it's gone for ever.

SUZY: Don't give up hope, Mr Passserby. We'll listen out for you. Won't we, Neville?

2ND NARRATOR: But Neville secretly thought Mr Passerby was a bit of a liar.

(NEVILLE *growls*.)

MR PASSERBY: What sort of dog is that, anyway?

SUZY: He's a Pedigree Old English Wolf Boxer.

MR PASSERBY: Oh, yes?

1ST NARRATOR: I don't think Mr Passerby believed Suzy, either.

2ND NARRATOR: But one of the good things about visiting Mr Passerby was that he always had a very large supply of chocolate cake. And if there was one thing Neville was particularly partial to, it was chocolate cake.

1ST NARRATOR: Suzy quite liked it, too.

2ND NARRATOR: So while the two of them sat eating chocolate cake, Mr Passerby would grow sadder and sadder and finally he would start to sing to them as if hoping that his voice would come back to him. But it never did.

MR PASSERBY: (*Singing very badly*) Early one morning,
Just as the sun was rising,
I heard a maiden singing in the valley below.
Oh, don't deceive me
Oh, never leave me,
How could you treat a poor maiden so?

1ST NARRATOR: And although Mr Passerby tried his best, because after all it wasn't his fault, was it, if someone had stolen his voice, he really did make a dreadful racket.

2ND NARRATOR: It was all Suzy and Neville could do to stop laughing.

1ST NARRATOR: But Suzy was always very polite.

SUZY: That was very good, Mr Passerby.

(NEVILLE *makes a moaning sound*.)

1ST NARRATOR: Even if Neville wasn't.

MR PASSERBY: That's very kind of you to say so, Suzy, but it was terrible. Shall I sing you some more?

NEVILLE: (*Alarmed*) Woof! Woof! Woof!

SUZY: No, that's very kind of you, Mr Passerby, but I think we should be getting home now. Thank you for the cake.

MR PASSERBY: All right. Goodbye then. See you soon.

SUZY: Goodbye. We'll keep a look-out for your voice.

MR PASSERBY: Well, that's kind. But you'll never find it. Not now.

(MR PASSERBY *goes off*.)

2ND NARRATOR: But Neville started wondering what on earth a voice looked like anyway. And if he'd recognize one even if he saw it.

1ST NARRATOR: But he had a quick sniff round just in case.

(NEVILLE *snuffles about*.)

2ND NARRATOR: But he didn't find anything.

1ST NARRATOR: Unless you count a half-eaten toffee . . .

2ND NARRATOR: A matchbox . . .

1ST NARRATOR: One navy blue sock . . .

2ND NARRATOR: And a piece of chewed string.

SUZY: Neville, come on!

NEVILLE: Woof!

(NEVILLE *goes to follow* SUZY *off. The lights dim again. They both sit together on the porch, as before*.)

1ST NARRATOR: One evening, though, something very strange happened.

2ND NARRATOR: Suzy and Neville were sitting on the porch as usual after supper, watching the sky and thinking their thoughts, when suddenly . . .

SUZY: Neville!

NEVILLE: (*Startled*) Woof!

SUZY: Look! At the old house opposite. I thought I saw a light. Yes. Look. No, it's gone now. There was one, though. I'm sure there was. A minute ago . . .

(MOTHER *comes out.*)

MOTHER: Come on, you two. Bed-time.

SUZY: Mum, I saw a light . . .

MOTHER: A light? Where?

SUZY: In the old house. In one of the rooms on the top floor. One of the window shutters was loose and there was this light. Like a torch or a candle.

MOTHER: Don't be so silly, Suzy, you can't have done. The place hasn't been opened for years. It's all shutterduttered up.

SUZY: I know someone was there . . .

MOTHER: You've got too much imaginagination, that's your trouble, my girl. Come on, in you come. No stories for you tonight. Say goodnight to Neville.

SUZY: 'Night, Neville.

NEVILLE: Woof!

SUZY: Mum, do you think it's possible for someone to steal your voice during the night . . . ?

MOTHER: Steal it?

SUZY: Mr Passerby said that somebody stole his voice. While he was asleep. In Portugal. Or Paris. Or Peru.

MOTHER: I wouldn't believe too much Mr Passerasserby tells you. He drinks a lot more than's good for him, if you ask me . . .

SUZY: He used to be a famous opera singer . . .

MOTHER: Well, if he's an opera singer, I'm the Queen of Outer Mongonolia . . .

(MOTHER *goes in.*)

SUZY: (*Looking back, as she goes*) I know I saw a light . . .

(SUZY *goes in.*)

1ST NARRATOR: That night Neville sat up especially alert, watching the old house . . .

2ND NARRATOR: But although he watched very carefully and never once dozed off . . .

(NEVILLE *dozes off.*)

15

Well, maybe once . . .
(NEVILLE *jolts awake*.)
He saw nothing at all.

1ST NARRATOR: Next day after school, Suzy and Neville went to play in the garden of the old house as usual. They also wanted to look round.

(*Birdsong*.)

2ND NARRATOR: Neville ran about everywhere looking for clues.

SUZY: Found anything, Neville?

(NEVILLE *looks doubtful*.)

I certainly saw something last night. Look, you see. It was that window, right up there . . . In the high tower. Oh, well . . .

1ST NARRATOR: But suddenly, Neville saw something . . .

(NEVILLE *bounds to and fro excitedly, trying to point something out to* SUZY.)

SUZY: What is it, Neville? What have you found . . . ?

NEVILLE: Woof!

2ND NARRATOR: And Suzy saw what Neville had discovered. The old front door that was usually nailed up had been unsealed. The hinges had been oiled and it had a big new shiny lock.

SUZY: Someone has been here. I knew it.

NEVILLE: Woof!

1ST NARRATOR: And Suzy hurried home to tell her mother.

(*Birdsong fades.* MR PASSERBY *enters*.)

MR PASSERBY: Evening, Suzy, evening, Neville. Where are you off to in such a hurry?

SUZY: Someone's been inside the old house. There's a new lock on the door. We've just seen it.

MR PASSERBY: Yes, I heard a rumour. I heard there was someone interested in buying it.

SUZY: Who?

MR PASSERBY: Don't know. Someone rich. Or mad. Have to be to buy a house that size.

SUZY: I wonder who it could be. A millionaire?

MR PASSERBY: Got over fifty rooms, that house. Plus the cellars and the attics and the tower and the secret passages. It's even got a secret room, so they say. Fifty rooms. I used to have a house that size. When I was a famous opera singer.

SUZY: Really?

MR PASSERBY: In fact, I had four houses that size.

(NEVILLE *growls*.)

Well, three, anyway. One in San Francisco. That's in America. One in Turin. That's in Italy. One in Barcelona. That's in France.

SUZY: I thought Barcelona was in Spain.

MR PASSERBY: Yes, there's one there as well. See you later. I must just drop in for a quick glass of liquid refreshment. I've bought a new chocolate cake. Come round some time . . .

NEVILLE: Woof!

SUZY: We will. Bye.

2ND NARRATOR: So while Mr Passerby went off to the pub, Suzy and Neville went home to tell Mother their news. But when they got there, Mother was full of some very exciting news of her own . . .

SUZY: } Mum! Guess what we've . . .

(*Together*)

MOTHER: } Suzy! You'll never guess what . . .

MOTHER: No, you must hear my news first. They've just phoned me. I'm going to be promoted.

SUZY: Promoted!

MOTHER: To manage the biscuit shop. They've offered me the job.

SUZY: Mum!

NEVILLE: (*Celebrating*) Woof! Woof! Woof!

MOTHER: It'll mean a lot more money for us . . .

SUZY: I'm so pleased . . .

MOTHER: I'm going to cook us all a special supper, as a celebratiation . . .

SUZY: I'll help you . . .

1ST NARRATOR: And they were all, quite understandably, so excited that Suzy and Neville forgot all about their discovery at the old house.

2ND NARRATOR: After supper they all sat outside on the porch for a while.

MOTHER: What are you looking at, Suzy . . . ?

1ST NARRATOR: Suzy didn't like to tell her mother that she was looking up as she always did to see if she could see her father's balloon. Because she knew if she started talking about Father, she'd upset her mother. And it had been such a happy evening . . .

2ND NARRATOR: So instead she said . . .

SUZY: I wasn't looking at anything, really. Just at the stars . . .

MOTHER: Not many there tonight. It's quite cloudy. I think it might rain.

(NEVILLE *whimpers*.)

SUZY: Don't worry, Neville. If it rains, you can shelter in the porch here.

MOTHER: Maybe, now I'm earning more money, we can afford to buy Neville a kennel . . .

SUZY: There. Did you hear that, Neville?

MOTHER: You'll be a house-owner, Neville. With your own front door.

1ST NARRATOR: And that reminded Suzy that she hadn't told her mother the news that someone might be buying the big house.

MOTHER: Really? Well, fancy . . . I wonder who'd want to buy that place . . .

SUZY: That's what we were thinking. I hope it's someone nice.

MOTHER: It'll be someone rich. I don't know about nice. Well, you'd better steer clear of it in future. No more playing in that garden.

SUZY: Why not?

MOTHER: Because they won't want you to. They're not going to want you and Neville stampampeding around their garden, are they?

SUZY: Maybe they won't mind . . .

MOTHER: Well . . .

SUZY: We can ask them. When we meet them. If they minded . . .

MOTHER: I can't see they're going to want –
(*A clap of thunder*. NEVILLE *howls and runs and hides*.)
Oh, dear. We'd better get inside . . .

SUZY: Neville . . .

MOTHER: Better bring him in, too. Just till the storm's passed.
  (MOTHER *goes inside*.)
SUZY: Neville, come on, did you hear that? Come on. Don't
  stay out there, or you'll be struck by lightning . . .
  (*Another clap of thunder*. NEVILLE *scoots inside, followed by*
  SUZY.)
  (*As she goes*) You daft dog . . .
1ST NARRATOR: Once inside, they settled down in front of the
  fire. And as a special treat, Mother told them a special
  story while the storm raged outside . . .
2ND NARRATOR: Mother told them a really creepy ghost story
  . . . Well, fairly creepy. It was enough to make Neville's
  fur stand on end a bit and even Suzy felt a little nervous.
  (*More thunder, outside*.)
MOTHER: And suddenly, they heard a floorboarboard creak.
  Someone was coming along the hall . . .
  (NEVILLE *makes a whimpering noise*.)
  And the footsteps came nearer and nearer.
SUZY: Yes . . . ?
MOTHER: And they both held their breath . . . And the footsteps
  came still nearer and nearer . . .
SUZY: Yes . . . ?
  (NEVILLE *makes another whimpering noise*.)
MOTHER: And then, mysterieriously, the footsteps stopped
  outside the door.
SUZY: And what happened then?
MOTHER: And they listened very, very quietly. Hoping
  whatever-it-was wouldn't find them. And then suddenly,
  in the silence, they heard –
  (*Three loud knocks on the door make them all jump out of their
  skins. Especially* NEVILLE. *Who then recovers and rushes round
  in circles barking*.)
NEVILLE: Woof! Woof! Woof!
SUZY: Who on earth can that be? Neville, be quiet . . .
MOTHER: No idea. Not at this time. I'll go and see. Neville!
SUZY: Neville!
  (*More knocking*.)
MOTHER: Just a minute, I'm coming.
  (*She opens the door. A gust of wind. She steps back, startled,*

allowing MR ACCOUSTICUS *to step into the room.* NEVILLE *growls.* SUZY *and* MOTHER *stare at him.* MR ACCOUSTICUS *smiles.*)

MR ACCOUSTICUS: I do apologize for startling you. Mrs Newbury?

MOTHER: Yes . . .

MR ACCOUSTICUS: And this will be young Suzy. Yes?

SUZY: (*Guardedly*) Yes . . .

MR ACCOUSTICUS: And I'm afraid I don't know this one's name. What a lovely dog.

(NEVILLE *growls.*)

And naturally suspicious of strangers. Quite rightly, quite rightly. May I introduce myself? Konstantine Accousticus. I'm to be your new neighbour. I've just purchased the house across the street.

MOTHER: Oh, I see. Oh. Well, come in. Please.

MR ACCOUSTICUS: Thank you. Just for a moment. I called literally just to say hallo. What a charming little cottage.

MOTHER: Thank you.

MR ACCOUSTICUS: Beautiful.

(NEVILLE *growls at him again.*)

SUZY: Neville!

MR ACCOUSTICUS: (*To* NEVILLE) Now, now, now. We're going to have to make friends aren't we, old boy? If we're going to be neighbours. What's your name, then?

SUZY: Neville.

MR ACCOUSTICUS: Neville. Well, I'll tell you what, Neville, I'll make a bargain with you. You don't growl at me and I won't growl at you, all right? (*He chuckles.*)

MOTHER: It's a big house you've bought there.

MR ACCOUSTICUS: Yes, very big.

MOTHER: A lot of work to do on it?

MR ACCOUSTICUS: Oh, yes.

MOTHER: Got your family moving in soon, have you?

MR ACCOUSTICUS: No. No, I have no family. Just myself.

MOTHER: Oh. It's a large house just for one person.

MR ACCOUSTICUS: I have a lot of bits and pieces, you know. And then again I'm looking for peace and quiet.

MOTHER: Well, it's very quiet round here . . .

(*Thunderclap.* MR ACCOUSTICUS *winces.*)

(*Laughing*) Except during thunderstorms, that is.

MR ACCOUSTICUS: Yes.

MOTHER: We won't disturb you, anyway.

MR ACCOUSTICUS: I'm sure you won't.

MOTHER: Can I offer you something to eat?

MR ACCOUSTICUS: No, no. Thank you. As I say, this was just a brief call. Perhaps, though, once I've settled in, you'll accept an invitation to dine with me.

MOTHER: Oh, well. We're not great socialocializers, but I'm sure we'd be very pleased to . . .

MR ACCOUSTICUS: Splendid.

(*Another thunderclap.* MR ACCOUSTICUS *winces again.*)

MOTHER: Terrible, isn't it? Got all you need over there to settle in?

MR ACCOUSTICUS: Oh, yes . . .

MOTHER: Milk? Sugar? Tea? All your basic necessessities?

MR ACCOUSTICUS: Absolutely everything. Goodnight, Mrs Newbury.

MOTHER: Goodnight Mr Accou – Mr Accou –

MR ACCOUSTICUS: Accousticus . . .

MOTHER: Accousticousticus . . .

MR ACCOUSTICUS: Goodnight, young Suzy.

SUZY: Goodnight.

MR ACCOUSTICUS: (*As he moves to the door*) Goodnight, Neville.

(NEVILLE *growls.*)

(*Laughing*) Oh dear, oh dear . . .

(*He suddenly bares his teeth and snarls back at* NEVILLE *quite fiercely.* NEVILLE *whimpers and dives under a piece of furniture.* MR ACCOUSTICUS *roars with laughter.*)

Goodnight to you all. (*He goes out.*)

MOTHER: (*Quite smitten*) Well, what a charming man. Wasn't he charming?

SUZY: I didn't think so.

MOTHER: No?

SUZY: I didn't like him at all.

MOTHER: Suzy, how can you say that?

SUZY: He gave me the creeps. Neville didn't like him either, did you, Neville?

(NEVILLE *growls*.)

MOTHER: Well, I don't know. You two, honestly. How can you decide you don't like the man? You've barely met him.

SUZY: How can you decide you do like him? You've barely met him, either.

MOTHER: Well, I happen to be a little more philanthranthrapopical than you two, that's all. I don't think ill of a person until I've a just cause. And I'll have you know I found Mr Accousticousticus extremely charming. I'm very glad we have him as a new neighbour and I hope we'll be seeing a lot more of him in the future, too. It's time for bed. It's stopped raining so you can go outside again now, Neville.

(SUZY *and* MOTHER *go off*.)

1ST NARRATOR: And Suzy went to bed wondering why her mother had become quite so cross about Mr Accousticus. Sometimes, thought Suzy, adults behaved in a most peculiar way.

2ND NARRATOR: And she went to sleep and dreamt that Mr Accousticus was barking and growling outside her door. It wasn't a very nice dream.

1ST NARRATOR: But at least she was asleep and so she didn't hear Mr Passerby returning from the pub.

2ND NARRATOR: But Neville did. And although he growled at him, he didn't bark. Neville was very used by now to Mr Passerby coming home in the middle of the night, singing.

MR PASSERBY: (*Singing*) Early one morning,
      Just as the sun was rising,
      I heard a maiden singing in the valley be – whoops . . .
(MR PASSERBY *falls over in the road*.)

1ST NARRATOR: Mr Passerby was even more drunk than usual . . .

MR PASSERBY: I appear to have fallen down the valley below.
(*Clambering up*) Oh, don't – deceive me . . .
      Oh, never leave me,
      How could you treat a poor maiden so?
Poor maiden. What a rotten way to treat a maiden.
Some people just don't know how to treat maidens . . .
(MR PASSERBY *staggers off*.)

2ND NARRATOR: But Suzy, who was asleep, saw and heard none of this. Nor did her mother, who was also asleep and also dreaming about Mr Accousticus.

1ST NARRATOR: But Neville saw it all. He saw Mr Passerby staggering home and he saw a dark figure in the shadows who was also watching Mr Passerby.

(MR ACCOUSTICUS *appears from the shadows*.)

MR ACCOUSTICUS: (*Singing softly as he goes*) Oh, don't deceive me,

Oh, never leave me . . .

How could . . .

(*He laughs to himself.* MR ACCOUSTICUS *goes off.* NEVILLE *whines unhappily.*)

2ND NARRATOR: Neville didn't sleep that night at all.

1ST NARRATOR: The following morning was Saturday and Suzy didn't have to go to school. She liked Saturdays especially. Her mother didn't always have to work most Saturdays either and that meant they could all spend the day together, the three of them.

(SUZY *and* MOTHER *enter*.)

2ND NARRATOR: But on this particular day, Suzy's mother said she had to go into town.

SUZY: Oh, Mum, why?

MOTHER: I told you, I'm going to have my hair done. It's about time I did.

SUZY: How long will you be?

MOTHER: I'll be as quick as I can. Though if I've got time, I might just look for a new dress as well.

SUZY: A new dress!

MOTHER: (*Irritably*) Well, don't sound so surprised. I don't often spend money on myself, Suzy. But I think I deserve something new occasionally. Surely you don't begrudge me just for once trying to look a little fashionashionable.

(MOTHER *goes in*.)

1ST NARRATOR: Suzy looked at her mother in amazement. She never usually behaved like this.

2ND NARRATOR: It was all very strange indeed.

1ST NARRATOR: So Suzy and Neville went for a walk on their own.

2ND NARRATOR: And because Suzy was thinking about her mother and wondering what could have made her quite so cross about nothing at all, she didn't notice where they were going.

1ST NARRATOR: Nor did Neville. But then Neville never did notice where they were going much.

2ND NARRATOR: And accidentally they wandered into the garden of the big house.

1ST NARRATOR: Quite forgetting there was now someone living there.

SUZY: Come on, Neville. Let's play hide and seek. It's your turn to hide.

(NEVILLE *whimpers*.)

Neville . . .

(NEVILLE *whimpers again and paws the ground, unhappily*.)

What's the matter? Why don't you want to play?

Neville . . . ?

(MR ACCOUSTICUS *appears, suddenly and silently*.)

Oh!

MR ACCOUSTICUS: Good morning, young Suzy.

SUZY: Good morning.

(NEVILLE *whimpers*.)

MR ACCOUSTICUS: Good morning, Neville.

SUZY: We're very sorry. We forgot that this was your garden.

MR ACCOUSTICUS: That's perfectly all right. Do you usually play here?

SUZY: – Er, yes, we used to.

MR ACCOUSTICUS: Well, please, carry on. Come here and play whenever you want . . .

SUZY: Well, thank you, but . . .

MR ACCOUSTICUS: You're both very, very welcome. Please stay.

SUZY: (*Retreating from him*) Yes, maybe another day perhaps . . .

MR ACCOUSTICUS: Just as you wish.

SUZY: Bye!

MR ACCOUSTICUS: (*Sharper*) Suzy!

SUZY: Yes?

MR ACCOUSTICUS: If you do play here, you and your friend, you must play very, very quietly. Do you hear?

SUZY: Yes.

MR ACCOUSTICUS: Because I can't be doing with noise. You see, I have very special hearing. I can hear everything very clearly, do you understand?

SUZY: Yes.

MR ACCOUSTICUS: For instance, at this very moment, I can hear you both breathing very clearly. So I'll always know when you're in my garden. And if you hold your breath, like you are doing, I'll still be able to hear your heart beating. As I can now, you see?

SUZY: Yes . . .

MR ACCOUSTICUS: Bump . . . bump . . . bump . . bump . . .
I can even hear Neville's stomach rumbling . . .
(NEVILLE *whimpers*.)

SUZY: He had a very early breakfast . . .

MR ACCOUSTICUS: Just remember. Very, very quietly. Because if there's one thing I hate, it's noisy girls with noisy dogs.
(MR ACCOUSTICUS *goes*.)

SUZY: Neville, listen . . .
(NEVILLE *listens*.)
None of the birds are singing.
(NEVILLE *gives a little howl*.)
Ssssh!

2ND NARRATOR: And Suzy and Neville ran out of that garden, just as fast as they could.

1ST NARRATOR: Once they'd got their breath back, they decided to visit their friend Mr Passerby.

2ND NARRATOR: Not *just* because they were secretly hoping he might have some chocolate cake to offer them . . .

1ST NARRATOR: Nevertheless, that did cross Neville's mind. After all, he had had a very early breakfast.
(NEVILLE *licks his lips*.)

2ND NARRATOR: But when they arrived at Mr Passerby's . . .

SUZY: (*Calling*) Mr Passerby! Mr Passerby! Are you at home?

NEVILLE: Woof!

SUZY: Mr Passerby!

(MR PASSERBY *comes out of his house. He looks very sorry for himself. He is well wrapped up and has a long scarf wound around his neck. When he speaks he is totally inaudible.*)

MR PASSERBY: (*Silently*) What do you want?

SUZY: Good morning, Mr Passerby.

MR PASSERBY: I can't talk to you today, I've lost my voice.

SUZY: What?

MR PASSERBY: I've lost my voice.

SUZY: What's the matter, have you lost your voice?

MR PASSERBY: I've just said I have.

SUZY: How did you lose it?

MR PASSERBY: In the night. I was asleep and when I woke up it had gone.

SUZY: In the what?

MR PASSERBY: Night. In the night.

SUZY: In the night? You lost it in the night?

MR PASSERBY: Someone stole it.

SUZY: Stole it? Who stole it?

MR PASSERBY: Someone did.

SUZY: But, Mr Passerby, nobody could really have stolen your voice. Not really. You've probably got a cold, that's all.

MR PASSERBY: I tell you it was stolen. How am I going to get it back?

SUZY: You'll get it back in a day or two, I'm sure. Don't worry. Have you got any throat sweets?

MR PASSERBY: (*Shaking his head*) No. I don't need throat sweets. I just need someone to find my voice.

SUZY: I'll see if I can buy you some throat sweets. See you later. Keep warm.

(MR PASSERBY *goes inside, talking silently to himself.*)

Good old Mr Passerby. Even when he's ill he still makes up stories. He'll be all right in a day or two. I don't think there'll be any chocolate cake for us today.

(NEVILLE *whimpers.*)

Come on, Neville. We'll go and buy him some throat sweets. Let's go home and get some money.

IST NARRATOR: But when they got there, just as they were going into the cottage, they heard a strange sound from across the street, coming from the old house.

(MR PASSERBY'S *voice is heard in the distance.*)

MR PASSERBY: (*Singing*) . . . Oh, don't deceive me . . .

SUZY: Neville, that's Mr Passerby.

NEVILLE: Woof!

MR PASSERBY: Oh, never leave me . . .

NEVILLE: Woof!

SUZY: It can't be, we've only just left him at home. Anyway, he couldn't talk.

MR PASSERBY: How could you treat a poor maiden so . . . ?

SUZY: It's his voice. It's certainly his voice. (*Realization*) Neville, it's his voice . . . He was right. Someone did steal his voice. Mr Accousticus has stolen his voice.
(NEVILLE *growls.* MOTHER *comes out of the house with a bunch of roses.*)
Mum. Listen, you'll never guess what's happened –

MOTHER: Ah, Suzy, I'm glad you're back. I want you to take these across the road –

SUZY: Across the road? Why?

MOTHER: I've picked these roses from the garden to give to Mr Accousticousticus as a housewarming present.

SUZY: Mum, I can't go over there . . .

MOTHER: Why ever not?

SUZY: I just can't. Please.

MOTHER: Suzy, don't be so silly. Do as I say.

SUZY: Mum, please . . .

MOTHER: Suzy, I'll get very cross in a minute. I've a lot to do this morning, I want to get into town.

SUZY: I can't go there. I can't.

MOTHER: Suzy . . .

SUZY: Mr Accousticus stole Mr Passerby's voice in the night, you see . . .

MOTHER: He did what?

SUZY: He stole his voice. We've just heard it. We heard his voice, didn't we, Neville?

NEVILLE: Woof!

MOTHER: Mr Accousticousticus's voice?

SUZY: No. Mr Passerby's.

MOTHER: You heard Mr Passerassby's voice?

SUZY: Yes.

NEVILLE: Woof!

MOTHER: At Mr Accousticousticus's.

SUZY: Yes.

27

NEVILLE: Woof!

MOTHER: Well, perhaps Mr Passerasserby is visiting Mr Accousticousticus.

SUZY: He's not. Mr Passerby's at home. He's lost his voice. Mr Accousticus stole it in the night. And now Mr Accousticus has got Mr Passerby's voice. We've just heard it.

MOTHER: Suzy! That will do. I've never heard such nonsense in my life.

SUZY: But . . .

NEVILLE: Woof! Woof! Woof!

MOTHER: And you shut up as well, Neville!

SUZY: Mum . . .

MOTHER: Suzy! I don't know what's come over you this morning. Very well, I'll take these over there myself. You can go into the kitchen and tidy up. And take that dog with you. What's the matter with him?

NEVILLE: Woof!

SUZY: Mum, you can't go either . . .

MOTHER: I don't want to hear another word.

2ND NARRATOR: And before Suzy could say anything, her mother had crossed the road and gone through the gates, into the garden of the old house.

1ST NARRATOR: And they saw Mr Accousticus letting her in through his front door . . .

2ND NARRATOR: And they saw the door close behind her.

SUZY: Oh, Neville, what are we going to do?

(NEVILLE *whimpers*.)

1ST NARRATOR: And they both waited for what seemed like hours and hours and hours, But was probably only minutes and minutes and minutes.

2ND NARRATOR: And then, to their joy, the front door of the old house opened and out came her mother, smiling at Mr Accousticus.

1ST NARRATOR: And, more important, still speaking.

MR ACCOUSTICUS: That's so very kind of you. Thank you.

MOTHER: Not at all. Goodbye . . .

MR ACCOUSTICUS: Goodbye.

(MR ACCOUSTICUS *waves and goes inside.* MOTHER *returns to* SUZY *and* NEVILLE *who greet her warmly*.)

SUZY: Mum . . .

NEVILLE: Woof!

MOTHER: I'm not speaking to either of you at the moment. I'm still very angry. What are you doing, anyway? Have you tidied the kitchen like I asked you to?

SUZY: Not yet, we were . . .

MOTHER: Well, do it this minute. As soon as I get back I've got a lot of baking to do.

SUZY: Baking?

MOTHER: I've invited Mr Accousticousticus to supper.

SUZY: Here? With us?

(NEVILLE *whimpers*.)

MOTHER: Now what's the matter?

SUZY: He mustn't come here.

MOTHER: Why not?

SUZY: He – he just mustn't . . .

MOTHER: Well, I'm sorry, but he's coming. I've already issued the invitinvitation and he's coming.

SUZY: Well, I'm not having supper with him.

MOTHER: Suzy, you can suit youself. As far as I'm concerned I think it would probably be better if you didn't. You can go to bed without any supper.

NEVILLE: Woof!

MOTHER: And the same goes for you.

SUZY: He can't come here.

MOTHER: (*Ignoring her*) Now, there's no time to lose. Come on. Look lively, come on.

(MOTHER *goes inside*.)

SUZY: (*Following her in*) But, Mum . . .

1ST NARRATOR: But there was nothing Suzy could say. Her mother was far too excited . . .

2ND NARRATOR: And Neville sat on the porch and wondered what they could do. Because he felt somehow that Suzy and her mother and he were in some sort of danger. But he didn't quite know what. But it had something to do with Mr Accousticus. He was sure of that.

1ST NARRATOR: And as he sat there, he saw Mr Accousticus come out of his big house and stand staring and smiling at their cottage. Just the way Mr Accousticus had stared and smiled at Mr Passerby the night before.

2ND NARRATOR: And Neville felt he should do something to warn Suzy and her mother. So as Mr Accousticus continued to stand there, Neville started to bark.

NEVILLE: Woof! Woof! Woof! Woof! Woof! Woof!

SUZY: (*Off*) What is it, Neville? Quietly now.

(MR ACCOUSTICUS *stretches out his hand and points a finger at* NEVILLE. NEVILLE *continues to bark but slowly all the sound is drained away, until he is barking entirely silently.*)

MR ACCOUSTICUS: Now, I warned you, didn't I?

(*He laughs and goes into the house.* NEVILLE *tries one or two more barks. To no avail.* SUZY *comes out with a bone.*)

SUZY: That's better. What was that all that barking about, just now?

(NEVILLE *tries to tell her.*)

What's that?

(NEVILLE *tries to tell her again.*)

SUZY: What's that? Tell me.

1ST NARRATOR: But try as he might, there was nothing Neville could do to warn her.

SUZY: Oh, you silly dog. What are you playing at?

2ND NARRATOR: And just as Suzy was about to give up and go and help her mother again, from somewhere across the road Neville and Suzy heard the most chilling sound they had ever heard in their lives.

NEVILLE: (*His voice, off*) Woof! Woof! Woof! Woof!

SUZY: Neville, that's you! That's your bark. Mr Accousticus has stolen your bark.

(NEVILLE *whimpers silently.*)

(*Hugging him*) Don't worry, Neville. We'll get your bark back. We'll get Mr Passerby's voice back, too. And we'll get the birds to sing again. Don't worry. We'll do it. Somehow we will!

1ST NARRATOR: And how they did all that –

2ND NARRATOR: We'll tell you in a few minutes.

1ST NARRATOR: See you soon.

2ND NARRATOR: See you soon.

PART II

The same. NEVILLE *is sitting gloomily on the porch.* SUZY *hurries in and out occasionally, busily helping her mother.*

1ST NARRATOR: This is the rest of the story of Suzy and Neville. And how they defeated Mr Accousticus . . .

2ND NARRATOR: And how Neville got his bark back . . .

1ST NARRATOR: And how the birds sang sweetly again . . .

2ND NARRATOR: And how Mr Passerby also sang again – almost as sweetly as the birds . . .

1ST NARRATOR: For the rest of that day, Suzy helped her mother get ready for the supper that Suzy wasn't going to eat.

2ND NARRATOR: Because Suzy knew that her mother was as good as her word and once she said something she generally meant it.

1ST NARRATOR: Not that Suzy minded. She didn't want to sit down to a meal with Mr Accousticus, not at all.

2ND NARRATOR: Neville certainly didn't. Though he wouldn't have minded the meal.

1ST NARRATOR: In fact, if he hadn't been such a nice, well brought-up dog, not to mention a Pedigree Old English Wolf Boxer, he would probably have gone right over there and bitten Mr Accousticus in the foot.

2ND NARRATOR: But being a Pedigree Old English Wolf Boxer as he was, he could never do that sort of thing – not even to someone like Mr Accousticus.

1ST NARRATOR: So instead, he sat on the porch very unhappily.

2ND NARRATOR: He couldn't bark at anything now.

1ST NARRATOR: He couldn't bark at moths . . .

NEVILLE: (*Silently*) Woof!

2ND NARRATOR: He couldn't bark at bats . . .

NEVILLE: (*Silently*) Woof!

1ST NARRATOR: He couldn't bark at owls . . .
(*Owl hoots.*)

NEVILLE: (*Silently*) Woof!

2ND NARRATOR: And worst of all, he couldn't even bark at cats . . .

(*Cat yowls.*)

NEVILLE: (*Silently*) Woof! Woof!

1ST NARRATOR: And if anyone happened to pass by the house, he couldn't bark at them any more, either.

(MR PASSERBY *enters, rather drunk. He is still wrapped up and is trying to sing – but to no avail.* NEVILLE *tries to bark.*)

2ND NARRATOR: It all made Neville feel very depressed.

1ST NARRATOR: When Suzy had finished helping her mother prepare the supper, she came and sat with Neville on the porch.

(SUZY *has done this.*)

SUZY: Neville . . . I think I've got a plan. Listen.

(NEVILLE *listens.*)

When Mr Accousticus arrives, we'll both have to pretend to go to bed. Then, as soon as he and Mum start supper we can creep across to the big house and see if we can get in. Through a window, or something. And then we can have a good look for your bark. And Mr Passerby's voice. How does that sound?

(NEVILLE *looks cowed.*)

Yes, I know it's frightening. I don't want to go into that house either. I'm frightened, too. But it's the only way, Neville.

(NEVILLE *nods reluctantly.*)

You're a Pedigree Old English Wolf Boxer, Neville.

(NEVILLE *straightens up.*)

They're the bravest dogs there are.

(NEVILLE *looks brave.*)

They're afraid of nothing.

(NEVILLE *prowls about sneering.*)

You can't frighten an Old English Wolf Boxer. It's impossible.

(MOTHER *comes out. She has her new dress on and looks very smart.*)

MOTHER: (*Sharply*) Neville, what are you doing?

(NEVILLE *jumps at the sound of her voice and dives for cover.*)

2ND NARRATOR: Suzy's mother had been to the hairdressers and bought herself a new dress. She was obviously very keen to impress Mr Accousticus . . .

1ST NARRATOR: But Suzy really couldn't understand why.

2ND NARRATOR: Her mother wasn't as cross with them both as she had been – after all, Suzy had helped her a lot with the supper –

1ST NARRATOR: But she was still a little bit angry.

MOTHER: He'll be here soon. Now, Suzy, since you've been so helpful, I'm going to forgive you and let you and Neville stay up for supper with us, all right?

(NEVILLE *perks up*.)

SUZY: No, thank you, Mum.

MOTHER: What?

SUZY: We don't want any supper, do we, Neville?

(NEVILLE *looks dubious*.)

MOTHER: Don't want any supper? You don't want any thick vegetegable soup?

SUZY: No.

(NEVILLE *looks increasingly desperate*.)

MOTHER: Or roast chicken with roast potatoes and peas . . .

SUZY: No.

(NEVILLE *bangs his head on the floor*.)

MOTHER: Or lemoneringeringeringue pie with ice cream?

(NEVILLE *rolls over in a desperate state*.)

SUZY: No, we don't, Neville, do we? Neville! We just want to go to bed early, don't we?

(NEVILLE *looks puzzled*.)

(*Pointedly*) Don't we? Neville?

MOTHER: Well, suit yourselves, you silly pair. Mr Accousticus and I will eat it all ourselves.

SUZY: I wish you weren't eating with him, either.

MOTHER: Suzy, I don't know what you've got against the poor man, I really don't . . .

SUZY: I've told you – he stole Mr Passerby's voice. And now he's stolen Neville's bark.

MOTHER: And I've told you – Mr Passerasserby has probably got a cold and Neville, thank goodness, has grown up a little and decided not to bark at everything in sight.

SUZY: What about the birds, then? Listen, they've stopped singing in the garden of the old house.

MOTHER: Because it's nearly night time, Suzy, they've gone to sleep.

SUZY: Oh, why won't you believe me?

MOTHER: Because I think you're making it all up. For some extraordinary reason you've decided you don't like Mr Accousticousticus. But I can't for the life of me see why. He's a charming, kind, educated man. And he's – very good-looking . . .

SUZY: Oh, Mum. What about Dad?

MOTHER: Your father's gone, dear. He's gone for ever. He went up in that stupid balloon and he's never going to come down, let's face it.

SUZY: He might, one day.

MOTHER: No, Suzy. Never. It's been too long. And I'm sorry, if someone like Mr Accousticousticus wants to – come and visit me – well, I'm only human, Suzy . . . and I must say, I find him very . . .

(MR ACCOUSTICUS *appears. He, too, has dressed up. He wears a cape and looks even more dark and sinister than before.*)

MR ACCOUSTICUS: Good evening, ladies.

MOTHER: (*Twittering slightly*) Oh, Mr Accousticousticus . . .

MR ACCOUSTICUS: (*Kissing her hand*) Dear lady . . . You're looking a perfect picture. (*Turning to* SUZY) Hallo, young Suzy . . .

SUZY: (*Drawing away*) 'Llo.

MR ACCOUSTICUS: Good evening, Neville.

(NEVILLE *has skulked off into a corner.*)

Still not going to say hallo, then, aren't we?

MOTHER: Well, he's not barking at you, anyway. That's a good sign.

MR ACCOUSTICUS: No, he's certainly not barking any more. He's learnt not to bark, haven't you, boy?

(*He moves towards* NEVILLE *who draws back.*)

SUZY: (*Shouting*) Don't you dare touch him!

(MR ACCOUSTICUS *turns, startled.*)

MOTHER: Suzy, really.

(MR ACCOUSTICUS *stares at* SUZY *who is frightened by his look.*)

34

I'm really so sorry. Suzy, you know perfectly well, it's very rude to shout at people. Now apologize.

SUZY: (*Muttering*) Sorry.

MR ACCOUSTICUS: It's also very bad for you, Suzy. I knew a little girl once, she shouted so loudly she lost her voice altogether. You wouldn't want that to happen, would you?

MOTHER: There, Suzy. Be warned. Now please, Mr Accousticousticus, do come inside, won't you? Perhaps you'd like a glass of our home-made dandeandelion wine?

MR ACCOUSTICUS: (*As he goes*) Home-made dandelion. Yum-yum-yum . . .

MOTHER: (*As she follows him off*) Five minutes, Suzy. And then I want you both in bed. I've never seen such behaviour. Really, I'm ashamed of you both. You're like a pair of hooligooligans.

(MOTHER *and* MR ACCOUSTICUS *have gone inside.*)

2ND NARRATOR: Suzy and Neville sat on the porch and tried to pluck up courage to face their adventure ahead.

1ST NARRATOR: And as they sat there, Suzy may have dozed off a little – maybe she dreamed or maybe she didn't and maybe it really happened, we shall never know – but she thought she saw her father float past the moon, still in his balloon. And he seemed to call to her . . .

(FATHER *appears high up in his balloon.*)

FATHER: (*Calling*) Suzy . . . Suzy . . .

SUZY: (*Sleepily*) Dad . . .

FATHER: Suzy . . .

SUZY: (*Sleepily*) Dad, we need you . . .

FATHER: You have to be very brave, Suzy. Very brave.

SUZY: I'll try, Dad, I'll try . . .

FATHER: There's great danger ahead, so be careful. Be careful, both of you, do you hear . . . ?

SUZY: I'll be careful.

FATHER: But don't be afraid. You mustn't be afraid, Suzy . . .

SUZY: No, all right. I'll do my best.

FATHER: Remember, Suzy, wherever you are, I'll be near. I'll be watching you. Don't be afraid . . . (*Fading away*) Don't be afraid . . . Don't be afraid . . .

(FATHER *has gone.*)

SUZY: (*Calling after him*) Dad . . . Dad . . . Dad . . .

2ND NARRATOR: And her father seemed to float away from her, as if he were carried away on the night wind . . .

SUZY: (*Sleepily*) Dad . . . Dad . . . Dad . . .

(MOTHER *enters*.)

MOTHER: (*Loudly*) Suzy! Neville! Time for bed now!

SUZY: (*Waking up*) What? Oh, Mum . . .

MOTHER: Good gracious, girl. Are you falling asleep out here?

SUZY: No, I was . . . I saw Dad . . .

MOTHER: Suzy, come on. Time for bed.

SUZY: I did, I saw Dad, he was . . .

MOTHER: (*Kindly*) Suzy, you were dreaming, darling. You can't have seen Dad. I'm sorry. (*Kisses her*) Now go to bed.

SUZY: Yes, Mum . . .

(MOTHER *goes inside again*.)

(*Softly*) I'll be down in about half an hour, Neville. Now you keep awake. All right?

MOTHER: (*Off*) Suzy!

SUZY: (*Calling*) Coming, Mum! (Sotto, *to* NEVILLE) Don't go to sleep.

(SUZY *goes inside*.)

1ST NARRATOR: And Neville sat all alone, thinking that perhaps, on the whole, Suzy's idea wasn't that good after all and perhaps it would be better *not* to try and get into Mr Accousticus's house opposite because, after all, he didn't really *need* his bark that much, did he, I mean, after all, quite a lot of animals got along very nicely without a bark, didn't they, mice for one. And beavers. And voles. And camels. And then he found he was dozing off. And he stopped himself just in time.

(NEVILLE *jolts awake*.)

2ND NARRATOR: And in order to help him stay awake, Neville tried to think of a few other animals that didn't need a bark. Cows didn't.

1ST NARRATOR: And pigs didn't.

2ND NARRATOR: And fish certainly didn't.

1ST NARRATOR: And cats didn't.

2ND NARRATOR: And rats didn't.

1ST NARRATOR: And sheep didn't . . .

2ND NARRATOR: And sheep didn't . . .

1ST NARRATOR: And sheep didn't . . .

2ND NARRATOR: And sheep didn't . . .

(NEVILLE *starts nodding asleep*.)

1ST NARRATOR: And what with all those sheep, Neville started nodding off again.

(NEVILLE *jolts awake*.)

2ND NARRATOR: So he decided perhaps the best thing to do was to walk about . . .

(NEVILLE *does this*.)

1ST NARRATOR: But after a time this got rather boring, because he didn't dare go very far away in case Suzy came out.

2ND NARRATOR: Then he had a very good idea.

1ST NARRATOR: While he was waiting he'd dig up one of the bones he'd buried and have a little snack before they went on their adventure.

2ND NARRATOR: Now, the only trouble with Neville was that although he was a first-rate digger and an even better bone bury-er – well, all Pedigree Old English Wolf Boxers are, of course – he hadn't got an awfully good memory when it came to digging them up again.

1ST NARRATOR: So he sniffed over here . . .

2ND NARRATOR: And he sniffed over there . . .

1ST NARRATOR: And then he dug over there . . .

2ND NARRATOR: And he dug over here . . .

1ST NARRATOR: And there . . .

2ND NARRATOR: And there . . .

1ST NARRATOR: And there . . .

2ND NARRATOR: Until finally he'd dug up the whole front garden and was absolutely exhausted . . .

(NEVILLE *sits panting*.)

1ST NARRATOR: And it was only then that it came to him – of course, they weren't buried in the front garden at all. He'd buried them round the back.

(NEVILLE *looks around him ruefully*.)

2ND NARRATOR: Ah, well. Too late now.

1ST NARRATOR: Just then, Suzy came out very quietly.

(SUZY *comes out and surveys the scene*.)

SUZY: Neville, what have you done? You've dug up all the

lawn. And the rose bushes. And the herbaceous borders. Mum's going to be furious. You mad dog.

(NEVILLE *looks suitably shame-faced.*)

Come on, then. Are you ready?

(*Voices are heard from the house.* MOTHER'*s laugh, then* MR ACCOUSTICUS'*s.*)

MOTHER: (*Off*) Oh, Mr Accousticousticus, really. You're not to say such things . . .

MR ACCOUSTICUS: I meant it, dear lady, I meant every word . . .

MOTHER: You're just a wicked flatteratterer . . . More dandeandelion?

MR ACCOUSTICUS: An excellent year, dear lady, an excellent year . . .

(MOTHER *laughs again.*)

SUZY: (*Listening*) They're just about to start supper. Come on, we have to be quick.

(*They move away. It grows darker.*)

2ND NARRATOR: It was a very dark night. No moon. Just the stars.

1ST NARRATOR: Suzy and Neville crept through Mr Accousticus's garden and along the garden path till they reached the big front door.

(*They both stop.* NEVILLE *moves forwards to the door.*)

SUZY: (*Whispering*) Well, there's no point in pushing, Neville. It'll be locked.

2ND NARRATOR: But Neville pushed the door anyway and to their surprise the big wooden door swung open.

1ST NARRATOR: Oddly though it didn't creak as a door might do, instead it made this strange sound.

(*A strange 'oooh-ing' noise. They jump back.*)

2ND NARRATOR: But then, as Suzy and Neville were to discover, nothing in Mr Accousticus's house sounded quite as it should do.

1ST NARRATOR: Carefully, they stepped inside the dark hallway.

(**At this point, the 'search' part of the play begins:**)

SUZY: Close the door.

(NEVILLE *does so. The strange 'ooh-ing' is repeated.* NEVILLE *jumps again.*)

Sssh! We must be very quiet. Which way now, do you think?

2ND NARRATOR: And so began Suzy and Neville's search of the house. It was huge, with dozens of rooms, as Mr Passerby had told them . . .

1ST NARRATOR: Not to mention corridors . . .

2ND NARRATOR: And hallways . . .

1ST NARRATOR: And secret passages . . .

2ND NARRATOR: It was possible to get very, very lost . . .

1ST NARRATOR: So it's also possible that Suzy and Neville may need our help . . .

2ND NARRATOR: First to find where Mr Accousticus had hidden Neville's bark . . .

1ST NARRATOR: And Mr Passerby's voice . . .

2ND NARRATOR: And the birdsong . . .

1ST NARRATOR: And once they've found them –

2ND NARRATOR: – possibly our help to get out of the house again.

1ST NARRATOR: We're also going to need to be rather quiet.

2ND NARRATOR: Because Mr Accousticus is only just across the street in Suzy's cottage . . .

1ST NARRATOR: And you will remember he has such fine hearing he actually listens to people's hearts beating . . .

2ND NARRATOR: So shhh!

SUZY: Ssssh!

(NEVILLE *freezes.*)

Which way now? We can go further along the hall . . .

1ST NARRATOR: I think they should go that way . . .

SUZY: Or we can go through this door here . . .

2ND NARRATOR: No, I think they should go that way . . .

1ST NARRATOR: We have a choice. We can either go further along the hall . . .

2ND NARRATOR: Or through the door there. It's up to you to choose.

1ST NARRATOR: All right! All those who think they should go along the hall . . . Hands up!

(*A vote is taken.*)

2ND NARRATOR: Right. Hands down. Now, all those who think they should go through the door . . . Hands up!

(*Another vote is taken.*
The NARRATORS *announce the winning decision.*)

(NOTE: **At this point the route taken by** SUZY **and** NEVILLE **will depend on decisions taken by the narrators and the audience. The search part of this should be conducted as quietly as possible. Later, when the chase section starts (i.e. when** SUZY **and** NEVILLE **are discovered by** MR ACCOUSTICUS**), all hell can break loose.**

The rooms are of course imagined. So are some of the larger props, though small ones would be nice. The Cabinet of Sounds should be real. A large box with dozens of tiny practical drawers. This can be hidden in different parts of the house on different performances, thus keeping an element of surprise for perhaps even the performers and defeating know-all kids who've seen the show more than once. So, depending on the choice:

Along the hall: The Far Hall, p. 56
Door: The Blue Drawing Room, below)

THE BLUE DRAWING ROOM

2ND NARRATOR: And so they entered the blue drawing room.

SUZY: What a huge room!

(*They gaze around them.*)

Do you see anything, Neville?

(NEVILLE *starts to patter about.*)

Careful. (*Discovering something.*) What's this? It looks like a musical box . . .

(*Opens lid. The sound of sheep.* NEVILLE *leaps.* SUZY *shuts the box sharply.*)

What an extraordinary house. Nothing is what it sounds,
is it? There's nothing in here. Where do we go now? There
doesn't seem any way out. Just the windows, they're
boarded up. And the fireplace. I can't see any way out
here – unless we climb up the chimney . . . And I don't
think that would . . .

(SUZY *looks up the chimney as she speaks.*)

Oh, Neville, look. There seems to be an iron ladder here
– it goes up the chimney for ever . . . What do you think?
Neville? What are you doing?

(NEVILLE *is snuffling and pawing in the other corner of the
room.*)

There's nothing there, it's just wooden panelling. Come
over here. Neville . . . Neville, what is it, boy . . . ?

(SUZY *moves to where* NEVILLE *is.*)

(*Pushing*) Look, it's just solid wall, it doesn't . . .

(*A whistling sound. The wall opens.*)

Oh yes, it does. It's a secret panel. Neville, you're brilliant!
Clever boy!

(NEVILLE *looks pleased.*)

Well, which way do we go, then? Shall we go through the
secret panel?

1ST NARRATOR: That's the way I think we should go.

SUZY: Or shall we climb up the chimney?

2ND NARRATOR: That's the way!

1ST NARRATOR: All right! All those who think they should go
through the secret panel . . . Hands up!
(*A vote is taken.*)

2ND NARRATOR: Right. Hands down! Now, all those who think
they should go up the chimney ladder . . . Hands up!
(*Another vote is taken and a decision made.*)

(Secret panel: The Wine Cellar, p. 52
Chimney: The Chimney Ladder/Attic Bedroom, p. 42)

SUZY: (*After this has happened*) I hope we can remember the
way back, that's all . . .

2ND NARRATOR: And so they started to climb the chimney ladder. Suzy went first. Neville followed her. He found climbing ladders very difficult.

(NEVILLE *slips and slides a bit.*)

SUZY: Come on, Neville.

2ND NARRATOR: After all, ladders were never built for dogs. Especially not Pedigree Old English Wolf Boxers. They climbed for what seemed like miles.

SUZY: (*Rather breathlessly*) This must lead right to the top of the house . . . I can see some light up there . . .

(*A loud motor horn. They both nearly fall.*)

What was that? I think it was a bat. Neville, this is a very peculiar house. Bats that make noises like car horns, I'm scared . . . Hang on. We're there, I think.

(*She steps off the ladder into a small room.* NEVILLE *follows.*)

2ND NARRATOR: Eventually they both clambered out through another fireplace into a small attic room.

SUZY: I think this is . . . It's a bedroom. It's very small. Right at the top of the house. Yes, look Neville, you can see for miles. We're very high up. Look, there's our cottage. The lights are on. I hope they're both still having dinner. And I hope Mum's OK. Nothing in here, anyway . . . What have we got now? Just the one door.

(SUZY *looks through it cautiously.* NEVILLE *meanwhile sits down on the bed. A chicken noise. He jumps up.*)

It seems to lead to a children's nursery. Oh, well. No choice in the matter. Come on, Neville. The nursery it is, then.

(The Nursery, below)

THE NURSERY

1ST NARRATOR: And so, very carefully, they entered the nursery. There was a cot, a small bed. A doll on the floor

– all covered in thick dust . . .

(NEVILLE *turns the doll over with his paw. It strikes like a clock.*)

SUZY: Ssssh! There've been no children sleeping in here for years. No sign of your bark, either. Not that I'd recognize it if I saw it. But it must be somewhere. Not here though. Where to now, do you think? (*She looks about her*) There's a door here. What's through here? Masses of toys, Neville. It's like a playroom. Where else? What's this? Looks like a chute. Goes down a long way. Don't fancy sliding down there. Must have been for laundry or something. Or rubbish. Well, which way? The playroom?

1ST NARRATOR: That's the way I should go.

SUZY: Or shall we risk the chute. I don't fancy that, though.

2ND NARRATOR: Down the chute. That's the way!

1ST NARRATOR: All right! All those who think they should go into the playroom . . . Hands up!
(*A vote is taken.*)

2ND NARRATOR: Right. Hands down. Now, all those who think they should go down the laundry chute . . . Hands up!
(*Another vote is taken and a decision made.*)

(The Playroom, below
The Chute/Laundry Room, p. 46)

THE PLAYROOM

1ST NARRATOR: And so, very quietly, Suzy and Neville tiptoed into the playroom. Another room covered in dust . . .

SUZY: Nobody's played in here for years, either. Quietly, Neville, don't tread on any toys . . .
(*The sound of a snore as* NEVILLE *treads on something.*)
Neville! There's a door here that looks as if it leads outside. Yes, it does. On to a balcony. What do you think, Neville? I don't think this other door leads anywhere at all. No, it's just a toy cupboard.
(NEVILLE *trots over to investigate.*)
I think this is the only way. Come on, we haven't got much

time. Mr Accousticus will be back soon. And if he catches us, I dread to think what he'll do to us. Neville . . .

1ST NARRATOR: But Neville had noticed something odd. A draught was blowing from the cupboard. As if there might be a space behind it.

SUZY: What have you found?

(NEVILLE *has become very excited.*)

You're right. There is something. At the back of this cupboard. It seems to be hollow . . . Just a minute. Help me to shove . . . And, together, heave . . .

(*Both* SUZY *and* NEVILLE *push at the back of the cupboard.*)

Look out, it's going!

(*A peal of church bells as* SUZY *and* NEVILLE *crash through the back of the cupboard and land in a heap.*)

Done it! Now . . . I don't know where this leads. It's very dark. We've got a choice now, Neville. Through the toy cupboard or out on to the balcony?

1ST NARRATOR: I think the toy cupboard sounds more interesting.

2ND NARRATOR: I think they should try the balcony. It's too dark the other way. We don't know what's down there.

1ST NARRATOR: All right! All those who think they should go through the cupboard . . . Hands up!

(*A vote is taken.*)

2ND NARRATOR: Right, Hands down. Now, all those who think they should try the balcony . . . Hands up!

(*Another vote is taken and a decision made.*)

(The toy cupboard: The Loft, below
The balcony: The Balcony/Tower, p. 50)

THE LOFT

1ST NARRATOR: And so Suzy and Neville squeezed through the narrow opening and started to half crouch, half crawl along the pitch-dark passageway. They moved very slowly. Suzy was extremely nervous. And as for Neville – he was terrified.

SUZY: Stay very close to me, Neville. It's so dark. I hope there aren't any holes in the floor. I'll never be able to avoid them if they – oops . . .
(*She bumps her head.*)
Watch out, Neville! Low beams.
(NEVILLE *bumps his head.*)
Better crouch, the ceiling seems to be getting lower. Though I think I can see some light ahead. Yes, just a glimmer. Come on, we're nearly there, Neville . . . ouch –
(*She bumps her head again.*)
Watch out, mind that one!
(NEVILLE *bumps his head again, too.*)

1ST NARRATOR: Very soon they came out into a low-ceilinged room. They were up in the very eaves of the old house.

(At this point there is an opportunity for them to discover The Cabinet of Sounds – if it has previously been decided to hide it here. If it has, we go straight to the discovery scene on p. 66; if not then the search continues as follows:)

SUZY: It's just the loft, it's a dead end. We can't go any further. Oh, this is hopeless. This house is just so huge . . . We could search in here for months and not find anything. Even if we knew what we were looking for. We'd better go downstairs again. There's nothing up here. Except for rafters and pipes and chimney stacks. Oh, look. If you look down these pipes you can see right into the basement. I bet you we could climb down these, there's room.
(NEVILLE *backs away hastily.*)
It wouldn't be too difficult. We could slide most of the way. Be much quicker than trying to find the stairs. I'm sure we'll be able to get out at the bottom. Come on. Let's try it. Come on, Neville. It's all right. I'll go first.
(SUZY *gets hold of the pipes.*)
Look, it's dead easy. Follow me.
(*They start to climb down.*)
You see, if we take it nice and easily there's no danger at all, you see, Neville. Just very gently and we'll soon be

the-e-e-e-e-r-r-r-r-e-e-e . . .

(SUZY *slips and* NEVILLE *does likewise.*)

1ST NARRATOR: And suddenly they were both slipping faster than they cared to think about and Suzy was trying to cling on and Neville was grabbing at anything that was passing but the whole thing became faster and faster and suddenly they were near the bottom and Suzy was sure that this was the end of everything and Neville just closed his eyes and waited for the crash. (*Pause.*)

SUZY: (*Opening her eyes*) Neville?

(NEVILLE *nuzzles her.*)

(*Incredulously*) Neville?

1ST NARRATOR: And the miracle had happened and they'd landed on a pile of old sacking left there years ago by builders long since departed.

SUZY: You all right? Where are we?

(*They get up gingerly to look.*)

We seem to be in a cupboard. Yes. Come on, let's look around.

(*And the two emerge into the laboratory.*)

(The Laboratory, p. 50)

THE CHUTE/LAUNDRY ROOM

SUZY: OK. Here we go then. Down the chute. Hold on to your hat, Neville.

2ND NARRATOR: Which puzzled Neville a bit, because he didn't have a hat and never had had one. He just assumed that all the excitement had driven Suzy slightly mad. Anyway, he certainly didn't fancy hurtling down a laundry chute – with or without a hat. But before he could think of a good alternative . . .

SUZY: Here goes. Oooooh . . .

(SUZY *and* NEVILLE *hurtle down the chute.*)

2ND NARRATOR: Down and down they plunged, faster and faster. Neville had never travelled so quickly in his life. And he certainly didn't want to ever again, thank you very

much. The journey seemed to take for ages, until
suddenly . . .

(*They collapse in a heap. They both sit panting.*)

SUZY: Whew!

2ND NARRATOR: When they'd recovered sufficiently to look
around, they saw that Suzy had guessed rightly. They
were, indeed, in Mr Accousticus's laundry room. They
were surrounded by sheets and pillowcases and shirts and
socks. Mr Accousticus seemed to have a particularly large
amount of socks.

SUZY: I don't think your bark can possibly be in here. Where
next? We haven't got much time left. Mr Accousticus will
be back soon. And if he catches us, I dread to think what
he'll do to us.

(SUZY *and* NEVILLE *explore.*)

There's a door here. But it seems to be locked. Oh well,
that's that. No, hang on a minute. There's some writing
on the door. It's very faint. (*Reading with difficulty*)

'To make me open, you must say,

Twixt Michaelmas and Christmas Day,

How many eggs can a gander lay?'

How very odd. How could anyone possibly guess that?
Any ideas, Neville?

(NEVILLE *hasn't. Maybe the audience will have. In case they
haven't:*)

2ND NARRATOR: Suzy considered the problem for a
moment . . .

SUZY: I don't know how many eggs a gander usually lays. It's
probably a trick question, anyway. You're no help,
Neville. I bet you don't even know what a gander is. Well,
for your information, it happens to be a male goose. Not
that that makes any . . . (*Realizing*) Oh . . . Geese lay eggs.
Ganders don't lay eggs, do they? (*To the door*) Answer:
they can't lay any eggs.

(*The sound of a bird singing.*)

Yes!

2ND NARRATOR: For, at that, the door mysteriously opened.
But Neville, despite not knowing anything about geese or
ganders, had made a discovery of his own.

(NEVILLE *scratches about excitedly on the floor*.)
For in among the sheets he had found . . .

SUZY: What is it now, Neville? Stop playing about. What have you found? Oh. Wow!

2ND NARRATOR: Suzy was very impressed. For Neville had discovered a trap-door.

SUZY: Well done. You're very good at finding things, Neville. I hope this isn't locked. (*She tugs at it*) No, I don't think it is, but it's very heavy . . . Give me a hand, Neville. Heave . . .

(SUZY *and* NEVILLE *heave the trap-door open. As they do so, it moos like a cow*.)

(*Looking down*) It's very deep and damp. It looks like a well. I'm not going down there for anything. I'm going through this door.

1ST NARRATOR: And I think that's the way you should go.

2ND NARRATOR: But Neville seemed much more interested in the trap-door. Which was, in my opinion, more promising.

1ST NARRATOR: All right! All those who think they should go through the door . . . Hands up!
(*A vote is taken.*)

2ND NARRATOR: Right. Hands down. Now, all those who think they should go down through Neville's trap-door . . . Hands up!
(*Another vote is taken and a decision made.*)

**(The door: The Laboratory, p. 50
The trap-door: The Dungeon, below)**

THE DUNGEON

2ND NARRATOR: And so, having chosen the trap-door, Suzy very bravely decided she would go first. She clambered through the hole and searched with her feet for some sort of footholds. But she could find none.

SUZY: I'm going to have to jump, Neville. Wish me luck. One . . . two . . . three . . .
(SUZY *jumps and lands with a jolt.*)

Ah! It's OK, it's not that big a drop. Come on, come on, Neville, jump.

2ND NARRATOR: But Neville, who a minute or so ago had been all for going down there, now seemed to have gone off the idea.

SUZY: Neville, come on. Come on, I'll catch you. That's it. Come on, don't be so stupid . . . come on . . . Neville!
(*Business as she gets* NEVILLE *to jump down to her. They finish in a heap.*)
You're a great useless lump sometimes, Neville. Now where we are? Uggh! It looks like a – like a dungeon. I hope there's some way out . . .

(At this point there is an opportunity for them to discover The Cabinet of Sounds – if it has previously been decided to hide it here. If it has, we go straight to the discovery scene on p. 66; if not then the search continues as follows:)

2ND NARRATOR: Suzy and Neville looked around for some time but the only way in seemed to be from the hole in the ceiling where they'd jumped down. But it was far too high for them to climb out again.

SUZY: There must be some other way out. We can't stay trapped in here for ever. Push at all the stones, see if there isn't some secret door. This house seems to be full of those. (*Jumping*) Ah! And this dungeon's full of rats. Go catch it, Neville.
(NEVILLE *jumps.*)
Neville, you're a dog. You're supposed to chase rats, not run away from them.
(NEVILLE *approaches the rat, nervously. It runs away making a noise like a racing car.*)

2ND NARRATOR: Neville, whilst being perfectly happy to chase rats in the normal course of events, didn't fancy chasing ones that sounded like racing cars. Whoever heard of being run over by a rat.

SUZY: Neville, I've got it! Look!
(*Sound of a doorbell.*)
It's a secret door. I don't know where it leads to but it's

our only way out. Come on, follow me.
(*And they go through the secret door and into the secret room.*)

(The Secret Room, p. 59)

THE LABORATORY

1ST NARRATOR: And so they entered the oddest of rooms. Full
of jars and bottles and glass tubes. And wires and big
boxes of strange-looking gadgetry. And the strong acrid
smell of chemicals.

SUZY: (*Wrinkling her nose*) Poo!
(NEVILLE *snuffles fiercely.*)
I think it's a laboratory . . . Mr Accousticus's laboratory.
Now, surely we must be getting close . . .

**(At this point there is an opportunity for them to discover
The Cabinet of Sounds – if it has previously been
decided to hide it here. If it has, we go straight to the
discovery scene on p. 66; if not then the search
continues as follows:)**

(*They look around.*)
No. No sign of anything. I was sure we were going to find
it here, too. Now where? Up those stairs, I suppose.
Wherever they lead. There seems to be a door at the top.
Come on, Neville, don't give up now. Keep going.

1ST NARRATOR: But secretly, Suzy was beginning to doubt
whether they would ever again find Neville's bark. But she
didn't have the heart to tell him that, of course.
(*They climb the stairs and enter the kitchen.*)

(The Kitchen, p. 55)

THE BALCONY/TOWER

Sound of wind howling.

2ND NARRATOR: And so they opened the door and stepped into
the open air and on to the balcony. It was very narrow

and very high up. Suzy and Neville both felt rather giddy.

SUZY: Don't look down, Neville. It's a very long way to the ground. And this railing doesn't seem very strong either. Oh, I don't like this at all. I'm not very good with heights. (SUZY *and* NEVILLE *shuffle along side by side.*) There seems to be a tower just along there. We must try and reach it. Careful . . .
(*Business as they work their way uncertainly along the narrow ledge.* SUZY *slips.* NEVILLE *grabs her.*)
Aaahhh! Neville, hold on to me. Don't let go. Hold on! That's it. Good boy. (*Safe again*) Whew! I nearly went that time.
(*They reach the tower.*)
Right. Let's get inside the tower . . . Then we'll be safer, I hope.

2ND NARRATOR: And they stepped through the wooden door and into the tower.
(*The wind stops.*)
Looking out of the narrow windows, they saw they were now at the very top of the house.

SUZY: Well, I'm glad we're safely through that, I can tell you. Now . . .

(At this point there is an opportunity for them to discover The Cabinet of Sounds – if it has previously been decided to hide it here. If it has, we go straight to the discovery scene on p. 66; if not, the search continues as follows:)

Nothing. Completely empty. I felt sure we'd be lucky this time. Oh, Neville, what are we going to do? We're never going to find your bark, ever, are we?
(SUZY *and* NEVILLE *sit holding on to each other, miserably.*)

2ND NARRATOR: But as she looked out of the window she remembered the dream she'd had about her father earlier. How he'd told her to be brave and that he'd be watching over her. And suddenly she found her courage again.

SUZY: Come on. We mustn't give up. Not now . . . Look, there's a small door there that we haven't tried. On we

go. Let's find out where this leads to.
(*They go through the small door and into the loft.*)

(The Loft, p. 44)

THE WINE CELLAR

1ST NARRATOR: Stepping through the secret panel Suzy all but
lost her balance.
(SUZY *teeters,* NEVILLE *grabs her.*)
The passage ended almost immediately in a sheer drop. A
deep shaft that went down further than either of them
could see.
SUZY: Luckily, there's an iron ladder down one side. We'll use
that. How good are you on iron ladders, Neville?
(NEVILLE *looks dubious.*)
Oh, well. Here we go. I'll lead. Only try not to fall on top
of me.
(SUZY *climbs down with* NEVILLE *following her.*)
Nearly there, I think. Just be careful. The last few rungs
are a bit slippery, so watch you don't . . .
(NEVILLE *falls on top of her. They tumble.*)
Neville! Get off! Get off me! (*Looking around*) Well, where
are we? It's full of bottles. Bottles of wine. I think we're
in Mr Accousticus's wine cellar. He must drink an awful
lot. There's hundreds of bottles. Trouble is, there doesn't
seem to be another way out of here. There must be. Have
a look, Neville. Just racks and racks of bottles.
(NEVILLE *is snuffling about in one corner.*)
What have you found, boy? Is this a way out? But it's just
a solid wall of bottles . . . unless they move in some way
. . . (*Leaning on them*) . . . yes, Neville, look, they're
moving . . . Give me a hand.
(SUZY *and* NEVILLE *lean on the stack of bottles and shove
together.*)
And – heave! Heave! Heave!
(*They open the concealed door.*)
(*Breathless*) There! You were right. Well found. This is the

only way to get out of here – unless we go back. Follow me, then.

(The Cellar, below)

THE CELLAR

1ST NARRATOR: And so they made their way through the narrow gap in the bottles and found themselves in a much larger cellar altogether, full of all manner of rubbish and junk.

SUZY: What a mess. There's piles of things. Covered in dust. Nobody's been down here for years and years. I don't think we'll find anything here.

(SUZY *finds a recorder*.)

Oh, look. A recorder. I started to learn to play one of these.

(*She blows the dust off and plays a few notes. A gargling sound. She drops it nervously*.)

I don't like this house at all. Where to now? Neville, look, in this old fireplace, it's the bottom of another iron ladder. It goes straight up the chimney. I suppose it could be part of the same one we saw just now in the drawing room. We could try it. It's quite a climb though.

(NEVILLE *has found the door*.)

I see, you'd rather try this door, would you? It seems to lead to some stairs going up. So it's up, whichever way we go. What do you think?

1ST NARRATOR: I think they should take the door and the stairs.

2ND NARRATOR: No, they ought to climb the ladder.

1ST NARRATOR: All right! All those who think they should go through the door and up the stairs . . . Hands up!

(*A vote is taken*.)

2ND NARRATOR: Right. Hands down. Now all those who think they should go up the ladder . . . Hands up!

(*Another vote is taken and a decision made*.)

**(The door and the stairs: The Scullery, p. 54
The fireplace/ladder: The Chimney Ladder/Attic Bedroom, p. 42**)

1ST NARRATOR: Through the door they went and up some
dusty, narrow wooden stairs and entered a small bare
room.

SUZY: This must be part of the kitchens. It doesn't seem to
have been used much lately either. Old mangle. A sink.
Mops and brooms. Nothing very interesting here. This
door must go through to the kitchen. Yes, I can see the
stove through there.

(NEVILLE *has found another door.*)

What's this then, Neville? Another door. (*Trying it*)
Locked, though. No way through there. Oh, wait a
minute. There's some writing on the door. It's very faint.
(*Reading with difficulty*)

'To open this door just as quick as a wink,
  If it takes ninety minutes to fill up that sink,
  How full in an hour and a half, do you think?'

How very odd. How could anyone possibly guess that?
Any ideas, Neville?

(NEVILLE *hasn't. Maybe the audience will have. In case they
haven't:*)

1ST NARRATOR: Suzy considered the problem for a moment . . .

SUZY: Well, the only way we'd ever solve that is to start filling
the sink. And timing ourselves. Only we can't really spare
an hour and half to do it, Neville, I'm sorry. I mean that's
ninety minutes when we could be . . . oh . . . an hour
and a half . . . they're the same. An hour and a half is
ninety minutes. So if it takes ninety minutes to fill the
sink, it takes an hour and a half to fill the sink. (*To the
door*) Answer: It would be full. In an hour and a half it
would be full.

1ST NARRATOR: And, at that, the door mysteriously opened.
(*A bird sings.*)

SUZY: Neville, it worked. All right, which way? Through this
door?

1ST NARRATOR: That's the way I'd go.

SUZY: Or into the kitchen? I think that's the way you'd like to
go, isn't it? Honestly, Neville, what a time to be hungry . . .

2ND NARRATOR: I'd go into the kitchen, too.

1ST NARRATOR: All right! All those who think they should go through the door that was locked . . . Hands up!
(*A vote is taken.*)

2ND NARRATOR: Right. Hands down. Now all those who think they should go into the kitchen . . . Hands up!
(*Another vote is taken and a decision made.*)

**(Through the door: The Laboratory, p. 50
The Kitchen, below)**

THE KITCHEN

2ND NARRATOR: And Suzy and Neville entered the kitchen. It was a huge room with a vast stove and a simply giant table. Large sideboards were filled with dusty china and, hanging on the ceiling above their heads, row upon row of frying pans and saucepans and steaming pans and cooking utensils of all shapes and sizes.

SUZY: Neville, look at it all. You could cook a banquet in here.
(NEVILLE *looks hopeful.*)
But do you realize, there's everything you could possibly want to cook with and prepare with and serve up with – but no food. Not a scrap anywhere. Look. I don't think Mr Accousticus ever eats at all.
(NEVILLE *looks disappointed.*)

(At this point there is an opportunity for them to discover The Cabinet of Sounds – if it has previously been decided to hide it here. If it has, we go straight to the discovery scene on p. 66; if not, then the search continues as follows:)

SUZY: Well, there only seems to be one way out of here. And that's the way we came in. So back we go. Come on, Neville.

2ND NARRATOR: But Neville had found something much more interesting at the back of the stove.

SUZY: Neville! All you're interested in is food. Come on! He'll be coming back in a minute. Then what we do? This is our only chance. What have you got there?

2ND NARRATOR: Neville had discovered something really interesting. For there behind the stove, just where all the heating pipes went down into the basement, was a long-forgotten trap-door.

SUZY: Neville, well done. Will it open? Come on, let's give it a try. And heave . . . and . . . heave . . . Done it!
(*A small fanfare as the trap-door comes open. They stare down into the darkness.*)
It looks a long way down. Oh well, we've come this far . . .
(*And they continue on into the dungeon.*)

The Dungeon, p. 48

The Dungeon, p. 48

THE FAR HALL

1ST NARRATOR: And so Suzy and Neville proceeded along the hall, walking as quietly as they could. Which was difficult because the floor had a rather peculiar squeak.
(*The floor snorts as they walk.*)

SUZY: Sounds as if we're walking on pigs.
(*They stop.*)
You know, I do hope we're going to remember our way back. In case we need to get out in a hurry. There's a door here. (*Looking in.*) It's another room. All red. Shall we go in there? Or go on down this hall?

1ST NARRATOR: I think they should carry on down the hall . . .

2ND NARRATOR: No, they should go into the red room, that's a much better idea.

1ST NARRATOR: All right! All those who think they should carry on down the hall . . . Hands up!
(*A vote is taken.*)

2ND NARRATOR: Right. Hands down. Now all those who think they should go into the red room . . . Hands up!
(*Another vote is taken and a decision made.*)

(**Continue down the hall: End of the Hall, p. 57
Red room: The Music Room, p. 62**)

END OF THE HALL

1ST NARRATOR: And so Suzy and Neville carried on till they
reached the end of the long hall, where they arrived at the
foot of a large staircase.

SUZY: Well, nowhere to go but up, Neville. It's an enormous
house. I don't know if we're ever going to find your bark.
(NEVILLE *looks distressed.*)
But don't you worry. We'll keep trying, we'll keep looking,
Neville. Come on then, upstairs . . .
(*They start to climb. Strange sounds as they do so — a crowd
briefly cheering, then booing, then laughing — on every third
step.*)
Neville, I'll be glad to get out of this house. It frightens
me.
(NEVILLE *agrees. They reach the top of the stairs.*)

(The Landing, below)

THE LANDING

1ST NARRATOR: And so they reached the top of the stairs and
found themselves on the first landing. And facing another
long, dark passage.

SUZY: Oh, dear. We can hardly see where we are and I daren't
turn a light on. If Mr Accousticus should happen to look
out of the cottage window, he'd know someone was in
here. OK, on we go.

1ST NARRATOR: And they crept a little further along the landing,
until they came to a doorway.

SUZY: What's in here then? Looks like a bedroom —
(NEVILLE *makes to go on in past her.*)
Neville, where are you going? You can't go to sleep now.
I think we should go on down the landing.

1ST NARRATOR: I think Suzy's right.

SUZY: But you want to go into the bedroom, do you?

2ND NARRATOR: I think Neville's right.

1ST NARRATOR: All right! All those who think they should carry on along the landing . . . Hands up!
(*A vote is taken.*)

2ND NARRATOR: Right. Hands down. Now all those who think they should have a look in the bedroom . . . Hands up!
(*Another vote is taken and a decision made.*)

(Further down the landing: The Far Landing, below The Bedroom, p. 60)

THE FAR LANDING

1ST NARRATOR: And so they carried on along the landing. But it proved to be very disappointing. For they rounded a corner and –

SUZY: (*Disappointed*) Oh . . . It's a dead end. No way forward. We'll have to go back. Oh dear, we haven't much time left. We're never going to find anything at this rate . . . Come on then, Neville. Don't lose heart. Neville, what are you looking at?
(NEVILLE *is looking upwards.*)
What's up there? What can you see? Oh, yes. It's a trapdoor in the ceiling. But we'll never get up there, Neville. Not without a ladder. It's miles too high. Unless – what if I stood on you . . .
(NEVILLE *looks very reluctant.*)
Well, you can't stand on me, can you?
(NEVILLE *thinks he might.*)
No, you're much too heavy, Neville. I'll have to stand on you. Come on, stand here. Now, keep steady, keep steady . . . that's it . . .
(*Business where* SUZY *stands on* NEVILLE's *shoulders. A great deal of to-ing and fro-ing as they wobble and finally collapse in a heap.*)
Oh, Neville, you're completely useless. Why couldn't you hang on? I was . . . What's that?
(*A musical box sound has started.*)

1ST NARRATOR: But at that point, Suzy noticed something else.

In their struggle to get at the trap-door in the ceiling they had knocked against the wall at the end of the hall. They had evidently disturbed some forgotten secret mechanism, for this was now slowly sliding open.

SUZY: (*Awed*) Neville, look! The whole wall is sliding back. (*They stare.*)
Well, it's another decision, Neville. Do we have another go at climbing through the trap-door up there? (NEVILLE *doesn't look keen.*)
I think that's the way we should go, myself.

1ST NARRATOR: So do I.

SUZY: But you'd rather try the secret door, would you?

2ND NARRATOR: So would I.

1ST NARRATOR: All right! All those who think they should climb up through the trap-door . . . Hands up! (*A vote is taken.*)

2ND NARRATOR: Right. Hands down. Now all those who think they should go through the secret door . . . Hands up! (*Another vote is taken and a decision made.*)

(Trap-door: The Loft, p. 44
Secret door: The Secret Room, below)

THE SECRET ROOM

2ND NARRATOR: And Suzy and Neville stepped through the secret door and into the secret room.

SUZY: (*Awed*) Gosh. It sparkles . . . Everything's sparkling.

2ND NARRATOR: It was a room filled with treasure. Gold and silver and jewels of all colours, glittering and gleaming. Suzy and Neville just stood and marvelled. (NEVILLE *moves forward.*)

SUZY: Neville, don't touch anything. It doesn't belong to us. None of it's ours. We must only take what belongs to us. If we start taking things that belong to Mr Accousticus then we're as bad as he is. (*Wistfully*) It is beautiful, though. And I wouldn't mind betting he stole all this in the first place, anyway. Still. Two wrongs don't make a right.

(At this point there is an opportunity for them to discover The Cabinet of Sounds – if it has previously been decided to hide it here. If it has, we go straight to the discovery scene on p. 66; if not then the search continues as follows:)

A room full of treasure and nothing for us, is there? I wonder if there's another way out of here? Yes, look, in the corner. It looks like a lift. We could see where that takes us. Come on. Come on, Neville, there's nothing to be frightened of, it's only a lift . . .
(*They both get into the lift which takes them to the study.*)

(The Study, p. 61)

THE BEDROOM

2ND NARRATOR: And Suzy and Neville tiptoed into Mr Accousticus's bedroom. It was a large room, almost as big as Suzy's whole cottage. And in the middle stood the biggest four-poster bed Suzy had ever seen. It was very quiet except for the alarm clock by the bed which, instead of ticking, was quacking.
(*Sound of quacking clock.*)
SUZY: Don't think there's anything here. We could look under the bed, I suppose.
(*They both look under it from different sides.* NEVILLE *catches sight of* SUZY *and jumps in alarm.*)
It's all right, Neville, that was me. Well. Where to now? There're some windows here that seem to lead on to a balcony. We could go that way. Can you see anywhere else to look?
(NEVILLE *can, in another corner.*)
What have you found now? It looks like a lift. Yes, well done. All right, shall we take the lift? Or explore the balcony?
1ST NARRATOR: They should definitely take the lift in my opinion.
2ND NARRATOR: No, the balcony. Definitely the balcony.

1ST NARRATOR: All right! All those who think they should get in the lift . . . Hands up!
(*A vote is taken.*)

2ND NARRATOR: Right. Hands down. Now all those who think they should go out on to the balcony . . . Hands up!
(*Another vote is taken and a decision made.*)

**(Lift: The Study, below
Balcony: Balcony/Tower, p. 50)**

THE STUDY

1ST NARRATOR: As soon as Suzy and Neville stepped into the lift, the door closed and they started to go up. It was quite slow and the journey seemed to take ages. Neville, who had never been in a lift before, found it all quite terrifying and kept close to the floor. Even Suzy who, of course, had been in a lift before felt a little nervous as the thing jolted and shook and wobbled them about before finally shuddering to a halt. The doors opened and Suzy and Neville stepped out. They saw they were in a room half way up the tower of the building.

SUZY: This seems to be Mr Accousticus's study . . .

(At this point there is an opportunity for them to discover The Cabinet of Sounds – if it has previously been decided to hide it here. If it has, we go straight to the discovery scene on p. 66; if not, then the search continues as follows:)

Papers, books. And look at this book. *Sounds*. Volume sixteen . . . (*She flips through the book*) Rowdy men in pubs . . . Noisy women in supermarkets . . . Newspaper sellers . . . This shows he's got a whole collection somewhere. But where's the collection? We must find it soon. I know he's going to be back in a minute, Neville. Look, there are some doors out on to the balcony – let's try out there. (*And they go out of the french doors on to the balcony leading to the tower.*)

(Balcony/Tower, p. 50)

2ND NARRATOR: Suzy and Neville entered the red room.
SUZY: This must be the music room. Look, a piano.

(*She tries a few notes. A trumpet fanfare.*)

Well, I think it's a piano. Here's a harp.

(*She tries that. Drum sounds.* NEVILLE *has found a tin whistle.*)

What have you got there? A whistle?

(NEVILLE *tries to blow it. A crash of glass.* NEVILLE *drops the whistle.*)

SShh! Let's try that door. It's the only way out of here.

(*She tries it. It is locked.*)

What's this say? (*She reads something on the door.*)

'I won't let you in to dine,
Eat my food or drink my wine,
Taste my breakfast, sip my tea,
'Til you've sung a song for me.'

Oh, terrific! Does that mean we have to sing to open the door? I suppose it does. You can't sing, can you, Neville, poor old thing? Wait a minute. I can't think of any songs. I know – what about that one that Mr Passerby always used to sing . . . ? (*Singing*) Early one morning . . . just as the sun was rising . . . that's it . . .

(SUZY *has difficulty in remembering the words. Maybe the audience can be persuaded to help her out. If not she'll have to struggle through on her own.*)

I heard a maiden singing in the valley below,
Oh, don't deceive me,
Oh, never leave me
How could you treat a poor maiden so?

(*At the end of all this the door opens, with a burst of sweet music.*)

Look, Neville, it worked. Come on, then. Dinner is served.

(The Dining Room, p. 63)

2ND NARRATOR: Suzy and Neville entered the dining room and there they saw one of the longest tables they had ever seen. It was laden with plates and knives and forks and candlesticks . . . And all covered in layers and layers of dust and cobwebs.

SUZY: I wouldn't like to eat in here very much. Not on my own. And it's so dusty. You'd get mouthfuls of fluff. (*They examine things on the table.*)
Ugggh! Well, it doesn't look as if anyone's even been in here for years, let alone eaten in here. On we go then. We could try those windows. They seem to open and lead to somewhere. Yes, it's full of huge plants, out there it's like a jungle. I think it's what they call a conservatory. Shall we go out there, Neville? It looks rather dangerous.

2ND NARRATOR: Neville agreed that it did. All those bushes and great plants – it looked just the sort of place to meet savage, wild animals. Fortunately once again, just then, he found another way to go.

SUZY: What have you found, then? Oh, yes. It's a little concealed door. It's painted like the wall so you hardly notice it. Oh, dear. Another choice. Which way shall we go then? Through this door?

1ST NARRATOR: That's the way I think they should go.

SUZY: Or through the french windows and into the jungle?

2ND NARRATOR: That way sounds more interesting to me.

1ST NARRATOR: All right! All those who think they should go through the concealed door . . . Hands up!
(*A vote is taken.*)

2ND NARRATOR: Right. Hands down. Now all those who think they should go out through the windows and into the jungle . . .
(*Another vote is taken and a decision made.*)

(**Concealed door: The Pantry, p. 65
The Conservatory, p. 64**)

2ND NARRATOR: Suzy and Neville stepped out through the
windows and into the jungle. Well, it wasn't really a jungle.
It was really a conservatory. But all the plants had been
allowed to grow wild and overgrown and because it was
fairly warm in there, it was certainly the nearest Suzy and
Neville had ever seen to the African jungle itself. There
were one or two birds flying around that had obviously
become trapped in there. Birds with a very strange song.
(*The sound of bicycle bells flying to and fro.*)

SUZY: I hope there aren't any wild animals in here . . .
(NEVILLE *looks nervous.*)
Like tigers.
(NEVILLE *looks around him fearfully*.)
Or snakes.
(NEVILLE *jumps.*)
I don't like snakes at all. It is very thick, the undergrowth,
though. You can hardly see where you're going. Neville?

2ND NARRATOR: But Neville had somehow lost sight of Suzy.
And now Suzy had lost Neville.

SUZY: Neville? Don't be silly, Neville. Don't play games. We
haven't got time for that. If Mr Accousticus comes back
while we're here, we're in real trouble. Neville . . . Neville?
(*They prowl about for a bit. Then* NEVILLE *leaps out at* SUZY,
mistaking her for someone else. They roll about.)
Neville, stop it! It's me! It's me! Neville!
(NEVILLE *stops attacking her.*)
Don't ever do that again. I thought you were a tiger . . .
Now, how do we get out of here? If we ever do get out.
What's that in the corner over there? It looks like a
door . . . (*Moving over to it*) Yes, look, Neville. It's the
door to a lift. Come on, let's try the lift . . .

2ND NARRATOR: But Neville had plans of his own and was busy
pulling away some plants which were hiding a steep flight
of wooden steps leading to small door, high in the wall.

SUZY: You've found another door? Which way do we go then?
In the lift?

1ST NARRATOR: That's certainly the best way to go.

SUZY: Or through your secret door, Neville.

2ND NARRATOR: That's the way I'd go.

1ST NARRATOR: All right! All those who think they should go
in the lift . . . Hands up!
(*A vote is taken.*)

2ND NARRATOR: Right. Hands down. Now all those who think
they should go up the steps and through the small door
. . . Hands up!
(*Another vote is taken and a decision made.*)

(Lift: The Study, p. 61
Secret door: The Secret Room, p. 59)

(Lift: The Study, p. 61
Secret door: The Secret Room, p. 59)

THE PANTRY

1ST NARRATOR: So Suzy and Neville stepped through the
concealed door. And found themselves in a short narrow
passageway.

SUZY: Come on then.

1ST NARRATOR: It led to a small room, lined with stone shelves
and with a stone paved floor. For a moment Suzy couldn't
think what it was. Then she recognized where she was.

SUZY: It's a pantry. It's meant to be a place for storing food,
but there's nothing here at all. I don't think Mr
Accousticus ever eats.
(NEVILLE *sniffs around hopefully.*)

1ST NARRATOR: Suzy was right. Neville couldn't even smell any
food. The faint scent of mice and a couple of dead
cockroaches. But nothing that Neville would regard as real
food. And certainly no trace of chocolate cake.

SUZY: Not even a biscuit, let alone a bark . . . Let's see . . .
Where next? This door seems to lead through to – yes, it
leads to the kitchen. I think that's the only way out of
here.
(*She moves to go that way and nearly loses her balance.*)
Whoops! Loose flagstone here. Watch out, I nearly . . .
(NEVILLE *snuffles round it.*)

What is it, Neville? Is there something underneath it?
Well, I don't think I can lift that even if there is. It's solid
stone. It's very heavy. Unless we . . . (*Kneeling down to it*)
Wait a minute, I think it pivots. Yes, if I press on this –
side – help me, Neville – help me, don't just stand
there . . .
(NEVILLE *helps. Sort of. Together they manage to pivot the
stone.*)
Done it! Neville, look! It's a trap-door. Well, now we do
have a choice. Shall we try the kitchen or risk this trap-
door?

1ST NARRATOR: I think they'd be safer going to the kitchen,
that way looks too dangerous to me.

2ND NARRATOR: Trap-door's more interesting, though.

1ST NARRATOR: All right! All those who think they should go
through the door into the kitchen . . . Hands up!
(*A vote is taken.*)

2ND NARRATOR: Right. Hands down. Now all those who think
they should risk the trap-door . . . Hands up!
(*Another vote is taken and a decision made.*)

(The Kitchen, p. 55
Trap-door: The Dungeon, p. 48)

**(At this point the play's 'search' sequence ends. The
Cabinet of Sounds has been located and now appears
in one of the previously decided locations (the kitchen,
the dungeon, the secret room, the study, the tower, the
loft or the laboratory). The following is now played in
whichever one of these locations.)**

SUZY: Neville, look! Just look! That must be it. It must be.
(*They rush forward to examine it.*)
Careful now. It's all labelled, see. This is what we've been
searching for. (*She reads the drawers*) Aircraft . . . Alarms
. . . Amusement Arcades . . . Anti-tank Guns . . .
Applause . . .
(*She carries on reading.* NEVILLE *opens one of the drawers just
a chink. A loud burst of applause. He shuts the drawer again.*)

Neville! Babies . . . Beds . . . Bells . . . Bicycles . . .
Birds . . .

(NEVILLE *opens another drawer. A baby cries. He shuts it
again.*)

Neville, I've told you, don't do that! (*Moving round the
other side.*) Hey, look round here. Singing. This could be
where we'll find Mr Passerby's voice . . .

(*She opens several drawers one after the other. We hear several
singers in quick succession. None of them is* MR PASSERBY.)

There's dozens of singers. How are we ever going to find
Mr Passerby's voice?

(NEVILLE *opens another drawer. A very smart voice says:
'Hallo, hallo, hallo, old boy!'* NEVILLE *appears to swallow
this.*)

NEVILLE: (*Repeating this*) Hallo, hallo, hallo, old boy.
SUZY: Neville, put that back!
NEVILLE: Hallo, hallo, hallo, old boy . . .
SUZY: (*Giggling*) Neville . . . Put it back . . .

(*She opens a drawer. A chicken clucks.* SUZY *opens her mouth
and repeats the sound. She spits it back into the drawer.*
NEVILLE *opens another drawer and swallows the contents. He
makes a noise like ship's siren.* SUZY *replies with a toilet flush.*
NEVILLE *replies with a series of crashes in quick succession.*)

That's it! Come on, no more. If he catches us here, we've
had it. Come on, you try and find your bark and I'll try
and find Mr Passerby. Look under B for Barks.

(NEVILLE *hunts through the drawers searching for his bark.
He finds several barks and tries them for size – a very big
bark (too big) – a very small bark, etc. Meanwhile,* SUZY
continues her search. Finally, NEVILLE *finds his original bark.
He rushes about barking with it, delightedly.*)

Neville, you found it! Well done. Quietly now, quietly.
We haven't got much time. I still can't find Mr
Passerby . . .

(SUZY *searches,* NEVILLE *frolics. He opens a draw marked
'Cats' and barks at a miaow or two.*)

Neville! Will you please be quiet and come and help me.
You see, he's got it all listed alphabetically. It should be
under P for Passerby but it isn't here . . .

(MR ACCOUSTICUS's *voice is suddenly heard very loudly in the room. But there is no visible sign of him, not immediately.*)

MR ACCOUSTICUS: I think you'll find Mr Passerby filed under N for Nuisance, Suzy.

(SUZY *and* NEVILLE *jump. They freeze.*)

The same file where I shall soon have to put your voice, Suzy. Along with all the rowdies and nosy little people. Where you belong.

SUZY: (*In a whisper, to* NEVILLE) Mr Accousticus!

NEVILLE: Woof!

(MR ACCOUSTICUS *appears from the shadows. His voice is still loud and seems to come from everywhere.*)

MR ACCOUSTICUS: Been enjoying our little tour of my house, have we?

NEVILLE: Woof!

MR ACCOUSTICUS: Oh, I see Neville has his bark again. We'll soon have that back, don't worry. If there's one thing I hate more than rowdy children, it's rowdy dogs . . .

(*He starts to advance on* NEVILLE *who retreats, growling.*)

Come here, boy. Give us your bark then, there's a good boy . . .

SUZY: Neville, don't bark at him . . . Whatever you do, don't ba –

(*She breaks off as* MR ACCOUSTICUS *wheels on her.*)

MR ACCOUSTICUS: I think we might as well have that voice, too, while we're about it. Then there'll be perfect peace, won't there?

(SUZY *stares at him wide-eyed. Her mouth tight shut.*)

No? Oh well, never mind, I can wait. I don't think you'll manage to keep quiet for long, Suzy . . . Not knowing you. You'll have to speak sooner or later, won't you? All right, let's start by tidying up this place. Pick up all the barks and put them back tidily where they belong.

SUZY: Pick up . . . (*She quickly closes her mouth.*)

MR ACCOUSTICUS: (*Wheels on her*) Ah! Nearly got you . . .

(*Sharply*) Come on, get things tidy . . . and hurry up about it!

(*They start to tidy.* MR ACCOUSTICUS *watches.* NEVILLE *opens a wrong drawer. An alarm bell goes off.*)

(*Covering his ears*) Shut that up at once, you stupid animal, you've opened the drawer full of burglar alarms. I detest burglar alarms.

(NEVILLE *does so hastily. He looks apologetic.* SUZY *opens another drawer. The sound of road drills.*)

(*Covering his ears*) I said, don't do that, you wretched little girl.

(SUZY *opens another. Church bells.*)

(*In some pain*) Aaaah!

SUZY: Come on, Neville, open the drawers. Open as many as you can. Let all the sounds out.

(*They both start to open every drawer they can, feverishly. The sounds build as they do so. As many as can be added. Cacophony.* MR ACCOUSTICUS *runs from the room yelling.*)

(*Above the din*) Now, run for it, Neville, run.

(*They hurry from wherever they are. The Cabinet of Sounds disappears and the sounds diminish.*)

Now remember, we have to retrace our steps exactly, if we're to get out of here. Which way?

(Hopefully, this can be done by the audience with a little help from the NARRATORS. Thus, things they've climbed they must now descend, things they've descended they must now reclimb, rooms they have entered they must now revisit. It can all be done quite swiftly.)

(*As this happens and* SUZY *and* NEVILLE *dash from room to room,* MR ACCOUSTICUS's *voice can be heard, pursuing them as they flee.*)

MR ACCOUSTICUS: I can still hear you, you know. I can hear you both breathing. I can hear both your hearts beating. You can't escape, you know . . . You'll never escape from this house . . . I can hear you both. You can't hide from me . . . You can't escape . . . (*He laughs.*)

(*Finally the escape is over.*)

SUZY: (*Breathlessly*) Look, Neville, the front door. The front door.

(*They rush out into the night air. They sit exhausted for a minute.*)

69

We're safe. We're safe. Come on, Neville. Let's go home now.

1ST NARRATOR: And Suzy and Neville crossed the street and returned to their cottage.

SUZY: Mum . . . Mum . . .

2ND NARRATOR: But the cottage was strangely quiet . . .

SUZY: (*Nervously*) Mum!

(MOTHER *appears on the doorstep*.)

Mum, are you all right?

(MOTHER *opens and shuts her mouth but can make no sound*.)

Oh, no . . . Mum . . .

(*They hug each other*. MR ACCOUSTICUS *appears. He carries a small box*.)

MR ACCOUSTICUS: I think it's this you're looking for, isn't it, Suzy?

(*He holds up the box and opens it a fraction. From inside, the sound of* MOTHER'*s voice*.)

MOTHER: (*Her voice*) Oh, Mr Accousticousticus, you're just a wicked flatteratterer . . .

(MR ACCOUSTICUS *closes the box*.)

SUZY: You give that back. You give back my mother's voice or I'll . . . I'll . . .

MR ACCOUSTICUS: Or you'll what? Tell me . . .

SUZY: I'll . . . I'll . . .

(*Her voice starts to fade*. MR ACCOUSTICUS *starts to draw* SUZY'*s voice from her*.)

Neville, I can't . . . speak . . . Mother . . . I can't . . .

1ST NARRATOR: And just when it all seemed lost . . .

2ND NARRATOR: Just when it all seemed that there was nothing that Suzy could do . . .

1ST NARRATOR: Or her mother could do . . .

2ND NARRATOR: Or Neville could do . . .

1ST NARRATOR: Like a bolt from the blue . . .

2ND NARRATOR: Like a prayer from heaven . . .

1ST NARRATOR: Like a knight in shining armour . . .

2ND NARRATOR: Like the US 5th Cavalry . . .

1ST NARRATOR:
2ND NARRATOR: } (*Together*) Down came Father's balloon!

(FATHER *appears and lands on* MR ACCOUSTICUS, *knocking him flat.*)

FATHER: Sorry! Beg your pardon!

(MR ACCOUSTICUS *runs off terrified.* NEVILLE *chases him.*)

NEVILLE: Woof! Woof! Woof!

SUZY: Dad! Oh, Dad . . . (*She rushes to embrace him.*)

FATHER: Hallo, old girl . . . (*To* MOTHER) Hallo, old dear.

(FATHER *embraces* MOTHER *and* SUZY.)

Who was that chap I just hit? Is he all right?

SUZY: Oh, Dad, it's a long story. We'll tell you later. Where have you been?

FATHER: Sorry I was so long. Fault with the balloon controls. Luckily we had a huge supply of corned beef. Been living on that and rain water. Good to see you both. (*To* MOTHER) How are you, dear? You're unnaturally quiet . . .

SUZY: Oh no! Mum's voice. He's still got Mum's voice . . .

FATHER: Got her voice? Who's got her voice?

SUZY: Mr Accousticus.

FATHER: Who on earth's Mr A-whosicus?

(NEVILLE *appears carrying the box in his mouth. He drops it at* SUZY's *feet.*)

NEVILLE: (*Through clenched teeth*) Woof!

SUZY: Oh, Neville, well done. (*Taking the box.*) Look, Dad, I'll show you . . .

(*She opens the box.* MOTHER's *voice comes first from the box and then from her own mouth as it 'transfers' to her.*)

MOTHER: (*Her 'boxed' voice*) Oh, Jack, it's so good to see you . . . (*Her own voice taking over*) . . . we've had the most terrible time since you've been away . . .

FATHER: Very good, that's awfully good.

MOTHER: The dreadful man moved in opposite, I never trusted him from the moment I first saw him . . .

FATHER: That's excellent, that's marvellous. I didn't see how you did that at all. How long have you been rehearsing that trick? Terrific. Sounded exactly as if you were coming from the box . . .

SUZY: No, Dad, you don't understand . . .

MOTHER: No, you see, Jack . . .

NEVILLE: Woof!

1ST NARRATOR: But try as they might, they never really got Suzy's father to believe the story . . .

FATHER: (*Laughing*) Come on! I wasn't born yesterday. Just because I've been up in balloon all this time, it doesn't make me a ballunatic.

(FATHER *and* MOTHER *go into the house together.*)

2ND NARRATOR: Still, never mind. Suzy and Neville couldn't complain, really. Father was back and that was the main thing. And Mother was terribly happy too, of course.

1ST NARRATOR: As for Mr Accousticus, well, he was never seen around those parts any more. He moved away and his house stayed empty again for ever.

(SUZY *and* NEVILLE *move back to the garden during the next and start to play.*)

2ND NARRATOR: It seemed that when Suzy and Neville released all those sounds and voices from the cabinet, it made the place so noisy that Mr Accousticus couldn't bear to live there a minute longer.

1ST NARRATOR: So Suzy and Neville took to playing in the old garden again.

(*Birdsong.*)

2ND NARRATOR: And everything got back to normal . . .

1ST NARRATOR: A lot of the voices that escaped did manage to find their way home to their rightful owners. People who hadn't spoken for years, dogs who hadn't barked, cows that hadn't mooed, cats that hadn't howled, babies that hadn't cried, singers that hadn't sung, woke up one morning to find their voices had returned to them.

(MR PASSERBY *enters, singing in an operatic tenor.*)

MR PASSERBY: Early one morning, just as the sun was rising . . . Good evening, Suzy! Good evening, Neville!

I heard a maiden singing in the valley below . . .

(*He goes off, still singing. During the next,* FATHER *and* MOTHER *come out on to the porch and sit together.*)

2ND NARRATOR: Though Suzy suspected that certain people actually got voices back that had never really belonged to them in the first place.

1ST NARRATOR: And so – as happens in all the best stories . . .

2ND NARRATOR: As we hope it will happen in your lives, too . . .

1ST NARRATOR: They all lived happily . . .

1ST NARRATOR:
2ND NARRATOR: } *(Together)* Ever after!

THE END